Dedication

In loving memory of Callie's grandfather, Jack (Honey) Carpenter, who embodied biblical earning, saving, spending, and giving.

Laura,
Thank you for your investment in my life + ministry as my spiritual director!! I'm so thankful for you!

Callie

What Readers are Saying About *Money Talks*

Reading this content-rich, spiritually-endowed book was like receiving warm, personal mentorship for the journey of financial discipleship. Practical guidance is woven together with real-life stories into a beautiful pathway, guiding readers to God-honoring management of both possessions and money.

Rev. Sue Nilson Kibbey
Director, Bishop Bruce Ough Innovation Center

Money Talks is a winsome and engaging, intensely practical guide to faithful living with our financial resources. Building on a strong biblical foundation, Rosario and Callie tackle one of the truly vexing issues of our day and time – the use and abuse of our financial resources. I strongly commend Money Talks for use by a working pastor preparing sermons on the subject of money or for the Sunday School/small group leader who is trying to help students grow in faithfulness to Christ. The reader will be blessed and guided in concrete ways to move forward in their walk with Christ.

Bishop Mike Lowry
Resident Bishop of the Central Texas Conference

Drawing from scripture, sermons by John Wesley and their own life experiences, Callie and Roz help us explore in this book how to earn, save, give and spend in a way that puts God, not money, first in our lives. Money Talks not only teaches us God's principles of handling money, but also gives us practical advice of how to put those principles into action. The spiritual fruit surveys at the end of each chapter are part of the genius of this book. Don't miss them.

Mark MacDonald
President, National Christian Foundation Kentucky

Money Talks by Callie and Roz Picardo is one of the most Biblically based, spiritually encouraging, wisely practical, and genuinely helpful books I have ever read on authentic Christian stewardship. It is creatively focused on John Wesley's guidance on Christian earning, saving, spending and giving with insightful personal illustrations. Money Talks reminds us that everything we are and have belongs to God and by using these gifts wisely and generously we are able to grow deeper in our faith and trust in Christ.

Dr. Kent Millard
President, United Theological Seminary

Money Talks is a flawless work that brings discovery to God's plan for financial faithfulness and success. This book gives insightful grounding to the purpose, plan, and proper place for financial stewardship, while also providing practical steps for any ministry, organization, or individual that is serious about financial growth. Laced with real-life stories and relevant scenarios, this book is a must read, and will leave you inspired to maximize the potential of your financial freedom.

Bishop Sir Walter Mack, Jr.

Senior Pastor, Union Baptist Church

The topic of Kingdom Stewardship is oftentimes misunderstood in church. While there are those who feel that the health and wealth "name it and claim it" model is the path to take, others feel the best practice to use is to spend it while you have it. Both of these methods are fundamentally flawed. In their book, *Money Talks,* Roz and Callie Picardo provide practical biblical principles to help everyday followers of Christ tosteward money in these uncertain times.

Rev. Dr. J. Elvin Sadler

General Secretary - Auditor, The AME Zion Church

Money talks—but for those with ears to hear—God speaks louder! So many of us get caught in the hamster wheel chasing after money. But the world is not enough to fill the void created by the disease of "more." What if there is a way that our work can be sacred? What if earning money can be an icon that points to God, rather than an idol that points to ourselves? What if the key to money is in being a channel through which God's blessings flow into the lives of others? Roz and Callie Picardo have given the world a gift in this book. They embody the Biblical principles they share. Drawing upon the wisdom of John Wesley to "earn all you can, save all you can, and give all you can" they show us a practical way to faithfully put God's voice first, so our finances can flourish and bear kingdom fruit. This gold mine of a resource is required reading for pastors and their teams!

Rev. Dr. Michael Adam Beck

Director of Remissioning, Fresh Expressions US

MONEY TALKS

A BIBLICAL TAKE ON EARNING, SAVING, SPENDING, AND GIVING

CALLIE PICARDO &
ROSARIO PICARDO

Money Talks

A Biblical Take on Earning,
Saving, Spending, and Giving

By Callie Picardo & Rosario Picardo

books@marketsquarebooks.com
P.O. Box 23664 Knoxville, Tennessee 37933

ISBN: 978-1-950899-29-6
Library of Congress: 2021940024

Printed and Bound in the United States of America

Publisher: Kevin Slimp
Editor: Kristin Lighter
Post-Process Editor: Ken Rochelle
Cover Design: Djuna Shorter

Unless noted, Scripture quotations taken from the following version of the Holy Bible:

NIV

Other Scripture versions used with permission:

ESV

Table of Contents

INTRODUCTION

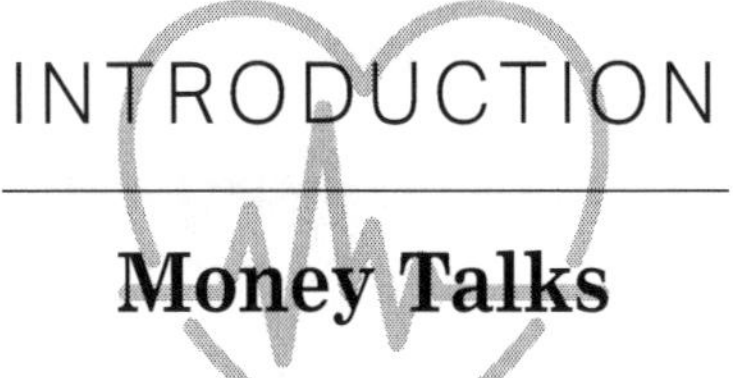

Money Talks

Money talks.

Money has power.

Influence.

It ascribes worth and value.

Almost like a god, money beckons us to worship and idolize. In fact, money has become a god for many of us.

We work and work to get more, buy more, consume more—to have the latest, the best, the better than we had before.

We stress about money. Will we have enough? What do we do when the bank account gets too low? When the credit card bills get too high? What happens when there's more month than money?

How much is enough? Will it ever be enough?

The good news is, money isn't the only thing that talks. God also talks. Even louder than money if we have the ears to hear.

God is the Word. He gave us the written word in the form of the Bible, but God is also speaking today through the power of the Holy Spirit. And as much as the world loves to talk about money, God has even more to say.

What is He trying to tell us in the midst of all this money talk? Simply this: He is enough.

The question for many of us is not what Scripture says about money (Jesus actually talks about money more than any other topic in the Gospels. Instead, it's how does the subject of money in Scripture apply to our everyday lives? While money is mentioned every single day throughout the world, it's often a neglected topic within the Church—aside from the occasional stewardship series.

So, how can we talk about money as it relates to our relationship with God, others, and the world? This book is spiritual—what we're after is a heart fully devoted to God—but it's also practical—"faith without works is dead" (James 2:26b), and talk without action gets us nowhere. Throughout these pages we'll explore how to actually earn, save, spend, and give in a way that puts God, not money, first.

There are countless Christian books on money, but many of them focus on worldly concepts—only attempting to fit God's Word in as an afterthought. This book is far from perfect, and as its authors, we, Callie and Roz, have been shaped by the context we've lived in—in this case the United States of America. All that being said, our hope is that in listening to God speak, we can let Him direct our steps in all areas— from earning and saving to spending and giving.

God doesn't need your money; He wants your heart, and

"where your treasure is, there your heart will be also" (Matthew 6:21).

That's why we're writing this book. Greed, materialism, debt, and consumerism have a hold on so many hearts, and we want to see people set free to worship God alone. It's nearly impossible to avoid the use of money in our culture, but it is possible to seek God first in all areas of our life and put money in its proper place: simply a tool used to give God the glory.

The truth is, this kind of mindset shift requires a complete worldview change. The idea of owning material things is a worldly concept that will mean nothing when you get to Heaven. We labor and toil for that which is temporary. So, what does it look like to spend what you have on things that last? To spend your life on things eternal? Should you give everything you have to the poor and live a life of poverty? Should you even bother to have a job? Is saving biblical? If you save, how much is enough?

Fortunately, God knows the answers to these and other questions, better than we ever could. He knew money would all-too-easily become an idol in our lives, but He doesn't leave us alone in this struggle. Instead, He gave us His Word.

There are over 2,350 verses relating to money, possessions, and finance in the Bible. God gave us Jesus as an example, and about 25 percent of all Jesus's teachings relate to money. Finally, when Jesus left this world, God gave us the gift of the Holy Spirit—a helper and advocate who's able to live in each of our hearts when we make the decision to accept Jesus as Lord and Savior. When we invite God into the secular, it becomes sacred. We want to encourage you to ask God to direct all areas of your life, including your finances, and watch what He will do.

In Galatians 5, the apostle Paul outlines the evidence that will be present in a Christian's life when you let the Holy Spirit be your guide. This evidence is referred to as the fruit of the Spirit:

> *But the fruit of the Spirit is love, joy, peace, patience, kindness, goodness, faithfulness, gentleness, self-control; against such things there is no law. And those who belong to Christ Jesus have crucified the flesh with its passions and desires. If we live by the Spirit, let us also keep in step with the Spirit.*
>
> **Galatians 5:22-25**

At the end of each chapter, you'll find a spiritual fruit inventory to help you discern where you're following God versus the world in that specific fruit of the Spirit. We encourage you not to gloss over those questions. Take some time to reflect, write out your responses, talk them over with your spouse if you're married, a Christian mentor, your small group, or an accountability partner. Really wrestle with the questions and invite God in. Ask Him to help you search your own heart for where you have listened to money talk instead of listening to His voice. Talk to Him about reorienting your worldview around His Word.

It all starts with surrender, and so we invite you even now to pray this prayer of surrender with us:

Holy God, I want You. I want more of You in my life. I humbly submit to You, and say 'not my will, but Yours be done,' in all areas of my life, but especially when it comes to finances. All I have is Yours. Forgive me for acting out of greed, envy, materialism, and lust for more. I confess that part of me is nervous to surrender it all to You. What might You ask me to do? But I also know how good You are. You gave up everything, coming to Earth to die on the cross for the debt of my sins, a debt I had no ability to pay on my own. So I surrender myself into Your loving hands. I know You love me unconditionally. Please guide me one step at a time as I seek to reorient my life, my priorities, my earning, saving, spending, and giving around You and Your Word. Thank You for Your abundant grace and Your Holy Spirit to lead and guide me. Amen.

CHAPTER ONE

The world's money says, "Chase Me." God's money says, "Earn Me."

Never spend money before you have earned it.

Thomas Jefferson

"Chase me!" the little child calls to a friend, and immediately the game of tag begins; back and forth, back and forth, changing directions until the pair of friends tire and move on to something new.

Money offers us the same invitation.

"Chase me! Chase me!" it calls, but just when we think we're about to catch it—so close to experiencing a win—money changes direction and we're forced to start again— chasing, chasing, continually in pursuit. Even when we think we're about to catch it, there's always more to chase when it comes to money. All too soon we get winded and start experiencing "the rat race of life." Rather than a fun game of tag played between friends, this rat race is more like running on a spinning wheel, expending lots of energy and never reaching a destination. It's a game that's far from fair and anything but fun.

God invites you to a better way of working. A way where you earn money through purposeful work, through serving God, rather than chasing money. Both ways—the relentless chase and the purposeful service—involve work, but the pace is different, the pursuit is different, and ultimately the posture of the heart is different. Both ways result in income, but God's way doesn't come at the expense of all of the people and things most important in your life.

Do you want your money to say, "Chase me?" Or do you want to teach it to recite a different script?

Money itself is neutral and work is a good thing, but today's consumer culture wants you to always be chasing money so you can spend, spend, spend. As a result, money can become an idol, something we chase and devote all our time and energy to winning. This kind of idolatry can lead to men and women becoming workaholics. It can result in gambling addictions for those who want to get rich quickly. And it can lead to us putting our value and worth in how much money we have rather than in God. That's why Paul warns in 1 Timothy:

> *Those who want to get rich fall into temptation and a trap and into many foolish and harmful desires that plunge people into ruin and destruction. For the love of money is a root of all kinds of evil. Some people, eager for money, have wandered from the faith and pierced themselves with many griefs."*
>
> **1 Timothy 6:9-10**

If getting rich and having as much money as you can is your goal, you will lose in the end. Someone will always be wealthier than you are. There will always be new toys to buy, new trips to take, new ways to get ahead. And in the end, money will not make you happy.

Israel's King Solomon is thought to be one of the wealthiest people to ever live. It's estimated that in today's dollars his peak net worth surpassed $2 Trillion.[1] King Solomon was also blessed with incredible wisdom. In 1 Kings 3, God actually appears to Solomon in a dream and offers him the opportunity to ask for anything he wants. Solomon could have asked for great wealth, for honor and fame, for revenge on an enemy, or for long life, but instead he asks God for wisdom so he could lead God's people well. Because of Solomon's noble request, God blessed him not just with wisdom, but with wealth and honor as well. It's out of this place of great wealth and wisdom that Solomon pens Ecclesiastes 5:10, "Whoever loves money never has enough; whoever loves wealth is never satisfied with their income. This too is meaningless." If one of the richest, wisest people to ever live found chasing after wealth meaningless, is there really a point in working to earn money?

Even before the Fall, when Adam and Eve were in the Garden of Eden, there was work to be done. After God

---

1 "The 20 Richest People of All Time," Microsoft News, April 25, 2017, https://www.msn.com/en-in/money/photos/the-20-richest-people-of-all-time/ss-BBsg8nX.

created Adam, God "put him in the Garden of Eden to work it and take care of it" (Genesis 2:15). Work is good. God has work for us to do, and just like God provided food in the garden for Adam and Eve to eat in return for their work, there is reward and compensation to be found for our work today. So how do we balance the blessing and need to work with the temptation to chase money?

The financial motto of John Wesley, the founder of Methodism, has become a favorite among preachers whenever they speak on stewardship:

Earn all you can, save all you can, give all you can."

In this first chapter, we're going to be looking at what it actually means to earn all you can. To really understand this principle, we're going to take a closer look at some of the general guidelines on how to earn an income found in Wesley's sermon, *The Use of Money,* based on the parable of the Shrewd Manager in Luke 16.

Earn all you can by honest industry, using all possible diligence in your calling.

The first guideline Wesley lays out for us is this: "Earn all you can by honest industry, using all possible diligence in your calling."[2]

---

[2] John Wesley, "The Sermons of John Wesley - Sermon 50, The Use of Money," The Wesley Center Online, accessed June 11, 2020, http://wesley.nnu.edu/john-wesley/the-sermons-of-john-wesley-1872-edition/sermon-50-the-use-of-money/.

What is God calling you to do? What does it mean to work for the Lord? Some Christians wrongly assume that really working for God requires following a call into ministry—becoming a pastor or moving somewhere "hard" to be a missionary. God does call some of us to a career change, but for many of us, that calling is staying right where we are and serving Him in our current circumstances.

When Callie was in college studying to get her business degree, one of the verses she committed to memory and recalled again and again was Colossians 3:23: "Whatever you do, work at it with all your heart, as working for the Lord, not for human masters." It was easy to work hard to get good grades and win the approval of professors and parents, but what did it mean to work with all your heart for the Lord? For Callie, it often meant getting up before her 8am class to spend time with the Lord, even if her homework wasn't done yet. It meant prioritizing church and Bible study over a major paper due on Monday. It meant taking a Sabbath (on Saturday in that season) to truly rest. That didn't mean school wasn't a priority. Callie studied hard, showed up at every class, and tried to really learn the material, instead of just cramming to pass the class. Working for the Lord instead of making school her idol meant trusting that God might use that work to give Callie a platform and prepare her for what lay ahead.

It also meant trusting God for His provision. Callie's senior year of college, she was offered a job in a bank management training program. She thanked the human resource department for the offer and then spent some time in prayer. God clearly said "No" to the job even though it was more money than Callie had ever made in her life. Instead of saying "Yes" to the wrong job, she trusted God to lead her to the right one. Later that spring, Callie received an offer as a financial analyst for an investment banking firm. As she prayed, she felt God saying this was the job she should accept.

Working for God doesn't mean the work will be easy. After graduation, Callie bought two suits and creatively adapted her wardrobe for her new role in the investment banking world. The days were long, and many coworkers spent weekends in the office. Callie kept working for the Lord, observing a Sabbath and trying to trust God with the steep learning curve. A few of her coworkers were Christians, but most were not. Callie didn't try to hide her faith. Instead, she shared God's love with her coworkers through her actions and by working hard for the Lord, giving her a platform at the firm.

British author C. S. Lewis, famous for his incredible children's fiction series *The Chronicles of Narnia*, was given a platform with Christians and non-Christians alike when he wrote about a certain lion, witch, and wardrobe. Originally published from 1950 to 1956 in London, the collection is now considered a children's literature classic with over 100 million copies sold in 47 languages. By far

Lewis's best-selling work, it has provided a platform for his Christian apologetics books such as *Mere Christianity.* His excellence in the literary craft then gave him more credibility when he shared the Gospel.

But even with that platform at work, there was still criticism to face for Callie. After a year of working harder than she ever had in her life, Callie had her annual review. It did not go well. She wanted to hear something similar to, "Well done, good and faithful servant." Instead, she heard, "We expected more when we hired you. We are giving you the minimum raise, but we expect you to do more."

Callie was crushed. As much as she tried to live to please God rather than being a people pleaser, those words cut deep. She had been working with all her heart, but it wasn't enough for her boss. It was hard to keep working. She started second-guessing herself and lost confidence in the work she was doing. When her boss walked past her cubicle, Callie could feel her level of anxiety rise. What did it mean to work with all her heart for the Lord when her human boss said it didn't measure up to his expectations? What did it mean when her anxiety was paralyzing?

One day as Callie was praying, she heard God say, "My beloved child, ask me for your annual review."

"Okay God," she replied, "How am I doing?"

God affirmed her worth, but also showed Callie ways she could be loving Him and others better through her work. That day Callie started praying for her boss. Instead of cowering when he walked by, she used the fear she felt as a reminder to start praying. As she prayed, her confidence grew. Instead of thinking through all the ways she could have responded to her boss during her review, she was proactively responding by praying for God to bless him.

If you bring your love for the Lord to the secular world, the secular becomes sacred. Conversely, you can work in the sacred world, but if you don't love God and your neighbor through your work, the sacred becomes secular. It's all a matter of the heart.

Callie's aunt, Sherry Leavell, realized this truth one day when she heard a preacher ask in a sermon, "Is what you do for a living a job, a blessing, or a calling?" Ever since Sherry was thirteen years-old, she had wanted to be a stockbroker, and that dream came true when she graduated from college, passed her licensing exams, and began work as a financial advisor. As a Christian, Sherry considered her job a blessing that allowed her to do ministry on the side. But it wasn't until she heard that sermon that she began to wonder if God had actually called her to be a stockbroker. How might the Lord want to use her in her current role? She prayed that God would show her how to integrate her faith more fully into her work, and she started praying regularly for her coworkers and clients. As she prayed for them, God began to show her ways to bless them with thoughtful cards and small gifts. Sherry had the opportunity to share her faith in her conversations and live in such a way that her actions witnessed to God's love. All of a sudden, her office became her mission field. Sherry's once secular job was reaching people with the love of Jesus Christ.[3]

Earn all you can without paying more for it than it is worth."

Another one of Wesley's caveats to "earn all you can" was, "Earn all you can without paying more for it than it is worth."[4] He goes on to explain that earning all you can should not be at the expense of life and health.

Wesley reminds us that there are things far more important than money. One of those things is your physical and mental health. There are jobs that, long-term, can take a toll on your health, even jobs in ministry. While some may be able to engage in certain work without harming their health, others, because of circumstances, boundaries, or a lack thereof, need to make a career change. A very dear clergy friend had to make such a change because of a heart condition—the stress of pastoring a church put her at a higher risk for heart attack or stroke.

The workload of Callie's first job in investment banking made her feel like she had to keep working until she couldn't work anymore. Fortunately, one of Callie's dear friends,

---

3 Sherry Leavell, "Our Calling," in *Grateful Living: 30 Days to Gratitude* (Louisville, KY: SL Publishing, 2018), p. 12.

4 John Wesley, "The Sermons of John Wesley - Sermon 50, The Use of Money," The Wesley Center Online, accessed June 11, 2020, http://wesley.nnu.edu/john-wesley/the-sermons-of-john-wesley-1872-edition/sermon-50-the-use-of-money/.

Anna, called Callie late at the office one evening and told her she needed to go home. When Callie protested, Anna firmly asked her, "If you stay late, will you get everything done on your to-do list?" Callie sighed, "No. I never get everything done." "Exactly," Anna replied. "You will always have more work to do tomorrow. Go home and rest."

Workaholism can quickly take away your health, marriage, and the relationships you are working to provide for. The truth is, work can easily become an idol. The thrill of making money, the excitement of closing a deal, the feeling of being needed—each of these factors can fill a need for worth that is unhealthy emotionally, spiritually, physically, and relationally. It's simply not worth it.

It might seem obvious, but our physical bodies were not made to work 24/7. As someone once said, "Working 24 hours a day for 7 days makes one WEAK." But at times it's hard to turn down incentives like overtime pay or a promotion, so instead we end up cutting other things in our life short—sleep patterns, family time, and our health—all in an effort to earn more.

Earning more at the expense of our life, family, health, Sabbath, and relationship with God is all in vain. The art of Sabbath rest is not just taking a day off, it's saying, "God, I trust you with all that I have and all that I am, and I know you will take care of everything else."

In the Bible, we first read about rest all the way back in the very beginning. Genesis 2:2 says:

By the seventh day God had finished the work he had been doing; so on the seventh day he rested from all his work.

God didn't need rest, but by resting on the Sabbath, God made it holy. As author Francis Frangipane points out:

Rest is not in the Sabbath; it is in God... the Sabbath was not a source of rest for God; He was the source of rest for the Sabbath.[5]

God gave us the Sabbath as a gift. It's a way to find our rest—our source—in God alone, not in our own ability to do more work. In the Ten Commandments, God directs Israel to rest. The Fourth Commandment says this: "Remember the sabbath day, to keep it holy" (Exodus 20:8, KJV). The first word, "remember," is important because human beings can be quite forgetful. "To keep it holy" means for this day to be set aside, more consecrated than other days. And there is blessing to be found in practicing Sabbath rest.

Isaiah 58:13-14 says:

If you turn back your foot from the sabbath, from doing your pleasure on my holy day, and call the sabbath a delight and the holy day of the Lord honorable; if you honor it, not going your own ways, or seeking your own pleasure, or talking idly; then you shall take delight in the Lord, and I will make you ride upon the heights of the earth.

Again, it all comes down to a matter of trust and seeking

---

5 Francis Frangipane, *Holiness, Truth, and the Presence of God* (Lake Mary, FL: Charisma House, 2011), p. 112.

God's kingdom first instead of building our own kingdoms. This is what Jesus is referring to in Matthew:

> *But seek first his kingdom and his righteousness, and all these things will be given to you as well."*
>
> **Matthew 6:33**

It's amazing how our needs are taken care of when we put God first and place our trust in Him.

But Sabbath can be extremely difficult for different personalities. Roz is an achiever by nature. It's hard for him to turn off work, especially since he's in vocational ministry and sees this as working for God. In Roz's single days as a church planter, it wasn't a big deal for him to be out every night of the week and work as much as he wanted. However, that same approach wasn't going to work when Roz got married and had three children. But he still tried to do it all—to be the best husband, father, and pastor.

Roz would spend time with everyone, and once the family went to bed he would go back to work and catch up on any administrative duties. Over the course of his ministry, he started to realize that work, even for God, had started to become an idol. Workaholism almost became a badge of honor. And even though work for Roz wasn't necessarily about the money, it still became his identity.

When COVID-19 hit in the spring of 2020, it became a time of soul-searching. We were both working full-time with two toddlers suddenly out of day-care and now at home.

Another baby was also on the way. Roz ended up losing 4-5 hours of work a day compared to his pre-pandemic schedule. But while preaching into a camera, little to no human interaction, and being quarantined with family for a few months was challenging, it ended up being the best thing for him. The quality time with family was something Roz will never forget, and it also helped him rediscover his primary identity as a child of God. Until you realize that your self-worth is not dependent on your net worth, role, or job title, all the efforts of striving and achieving are pointless.

Earn all you can, but not at the expense of your neighbor."

Another of Wesley's cautions about earning money over chasing money is this: "Earn all you can, but not at the expense of your neighbor."[6]

God's command to love your neighbor as you love yourself extends to how you treat your neighbor through your work. Remember, Wesley practiced and encouraged early Methodists to personal piety and social holiness. We cannot experience the fullness of God through rugged individualism and selfishness. Money can all too quickly become a point of tension and impede our relationships with others.

Even going back to the Old Testament, God directs Israel

---

[6] John Wesley, "The Sermons of John Wesley - Sermon 50, The Use of Money," The Wesley Center Online, accessed June 11, 2020, http://wesley.nnu.edu/john-wesley/the-sermons-of-john-wesley-1872-edition/sermon-50-the-use-of-money/.

to be different from their ancient near eastern neighbors. Deuteronomy 25:13-16 says:

> *God commanded Israel, "Do not have two differing weights in your bag—one heavy, one light. Do not have two differing measures in your house—one large, one small. You must have accurate and honest weights and measures, so that you may live long in the land the Lord your God is giving you. For the Lord your God detests anyone who does these things, anyone who deals dishonestly."*

Remember, your "neighbor" is not just the person who lives next door. The term applies to everyone you encounter. That means that in every situation we are not to cheat and never to take advantage of or rip someone off for personal gain. Gray areas may be acceptable in the world's eyes and in business practices, but our guidance and directives should come from the Scriptures. When we honor God by honoring others, it's amazing how God's blessings flow.

When money speaks from a worldly perspective, it says, "You need more. You need success, wealth, and fame. Make a name for yourself." God tells us to live for an audience of One. Money may give you more fans—people who want what you have—but that will not fulfill you. It won't make you happy. When you've lost it all, will those fans still be there? When you die, will what you built have any lasting value?

In 1888, a French newspaper mistakenly ran an obituary for Alfred Nobel, the wealthy inventor of dynamite. His brother was the one who had actually died, but seeing the words printed under the title "The Merchant of Death is Dead," caused Alfred to completely rethink his life. Eight years later when he did die, Nobel left $9 million to fund awards recognizing those who help humanity—the Nobel Peace Prize.[7]

Start with the end in mind. What do you want your own obituary to say about you? What will people at your funeral remember? Did you point anyone toward Jesus Christ? Did you make a name for yourself, or did you lift up God's holy name, the only One who can save?

Callie had multiple bosses in her role in investment banking. One was a strong Christian who took her under his wing and helped her grow in serving the Lord in the workplace. One day this boss called Callie into his office and kindly showed her how she was unintentionally dishonoring one of her coworkers.

With the workload at the financial firm, there was always more to be done in a day than could actually be accomplished. Prioritizing was also difficult with multiple bosses who all wanted their assignments done yesterday. The office administrative assistant was often willing to help lighten the load, but that required getting her what she needed for projects—a task often lower on Callie's priority list. Callie was so swamped with higher priority

---

[7] Randy C. Alcorn, "For Such a Time as This," in *The Treasure Principle: Unlocking the Secret of Joyful Giving* (Colorado Springs, CO: Multnomah Books, 2001), pp. 79-80.

needs she was repeatedly late getting the administrative assistant what she needed to help. At their meeting, Callie's boss gently brought the situation to her attention. Unintentionally, Callie was making this wonderful assistant feel unimportant and rejected when she was offering to help. She had no clue she was doing this, but her kind boss helped Callie grow and learn how to work better with her colleagues. In order to work for the Lord, she had to respect all of her coworkers, not just with her words, but also with her actions.

Wesley was vehemently against any form of slavery, even though the buying and selling of slaves was predominant in England at this time. He also stood against investing in companies that produced alcohol, tobacco, or gambling. Later Methodists added the avoidance of investing in weapon companies to this list. Wesley's basis for these purchasing restrictions was a popular general rule for Methodists: "Do No Harm." A love for God and a love for neighbor was the basis for how Christians earned and spent their money. If these early Methodists were engaged in what was perceived to be unethical ways of earning money, the result could be the unraveling of society's fabric. Earning a living by any means necessary would ultimately produce more harm in the world than good. In today's terms, this is known as being socially conscious in our employment.

Christians have often asked if it's wrong to gamble, even on an infrequent basis, such as the occasional lottery ticket purchase, slot machine game, or horse racing event that serves as more of a social gathering. And it really all depends on a few intentional considerations. The first being, what is your motive? Why are you doing this activity? Is it to earn extra money, or is it simply for a thrill? It's easy to develop a habit or addiction by trying to earn money the "easy way." Habits like gambling can start out innocently enough, but over time these habits can get out of control. There's a small thrill to winning $5, but the only time people mention gambling at all is when they win, not when they lose. Places like casinos are designed for players to lose more than they win—it's where we get the old adage "the house always wins."

The means through which you earn an income is more important than the money earned itself. If we truly believe everything belongs to God, do we think God will bless dishonest gain? The influence of gambling impacts more than the individual. It leads to a systemic issue within families and communities. As Proverbs 13:11 advises:

> *Wealth gained hastily will dwindle, but whoever gathers little by little will increase it."*

But what about the occasional Nickel card game with friends or, like we said before, an annual trip to watch the horse races where you buy a betting ticket? It's all based on one's interpretation of Scripture. If this kind of gambling is truly for fun, doesn't have a hold on you, and is something you can go without, then so be it. The apostle Paul tells us in 1 Corinthians 6:12:

> *"I have the right to do anything," you say–but not everything is beneficial. "I have the right to do anything"–but I will not be mastered by anything.*

As Christians, we have freedom in Christ. We can do anything, but who is that thing benefiting or hurting? The one thing to consider when gambling is your Christian witness in the world. Could these aforementioned innocent acts hurt any existing relationships you have or negatively influence the people you are trying to share Christ with? Only you can answer that.

Earn all you can, but not at the expense of your mind.

Wesley also cautioned, earn all you can, but not at the expense of your mind.[8] It's a matter of conscience, convictions, and maintaining integrity. The Holy Spirit desires to be our guide, even in money matters. When we ask for God's wisdom, God will not hold back. However, when we go against God's Word and act on our own accord to earn more, it's hard to find peace. In this scenario, making more money actually weighs us down and becomes a burden because our tactics are impure. Little white lies have the potential to snowball and become a big deal. This happens if we're dishonest when filing our taxes, fudge

---

[8] John Wesley, "The Sermons of John Wesley - Sermon 50, The Use of Money," The Wesley Center Online, accessed June 11, 2020, http://wesley.nnu.edu/john-wesley/the-sermons-of-john-wesley-1872-edition/sermon-50-the-use-of-money/.

our hours at work, or sell our old vehicle without fully disclosing things that we know are wrong with it.

There are also jobs out there that sadly ask employees to engage in activities that are unlawful or contrary to God's Word. Do not let desire or a need for money keep you in a business that requires you to act in ways that dishonor the Lord. That money may cost more than it's worth.

Employment has been hard to come by for some, leaving Americans to take jobs they otherwise wouldn't want and that are outside their skill-set or passion. What do you do when you feel like your employer is being unethical, engaging in something like tax fraud, or paying you under the table?

First and foremost, as followers of Jesus our first allegiance is to God. However, Christians are to lead by example, being upright citizens and submitting to the authority they are under when it comes to the law of the land. The apostle Paul carefully lays this out for us in Romans 13:6-7 where he says, "This is also why you pay taxes, for the authorities are God's servants, who give their full time to governing. Give to everyone what you owe them: If you owe taxes, pay taxes; if revenue, then revenue; if respect, then respect; if honor, then honor." We are called to live above reproach, especially if we want to experience and live in blessing. This of course means paying our taxes and prayerfully deciding to talk to an employer who is trying to cheat the system. But it can leave one with a difficult decision to make. The same applies when filing taxes. Are we honest in how we disclose our income? Are we trying to avoid paying taxes or earning a tax refund in ways that are illegal? Again, this all goes back to Paul's words about respecting and honoring those in authority over us.

In the same vein, there's the question of working a job that's promoting unethical or even immoral behavior. Again, "all things are permissible but not all are beneficial." One young lady that was coming to our church was starting to grow in her conviction that she no longer wanted to work at Victoria's Secret. This young lady prayerfully decided to end her employment at the store because she believed the company was propagating women as purely sexual objects. After some time, she decided working at Victoria's Secret didn't line up with her spiritual walk. While being employed was important for this young lady, she didn't want to contribute to the further subjugation of women, and in the end, God provided her with other employment.

Do you trust God enough with your finances to be fair, or even more than fair, with others? This doesn't mean we act ignorantly when it comes to making a deal. It also doesn't mean getting paid less than what you're worth in terms of fair wages. If any type of negotiation or relationship is one-sided it starts a precedent for one group or individual to be at a deficit. This uneven dynamic often plays out negatively later in the relationship. Instead of putting yourself down, the question to ask is what is a win for everyone involved? As a follower of Jesus, how do you value others and seek the best interest of all involved? There are a few wise sayings about this principle in the book of Proverbs:

> *Better a little with the fear of the Lord than great wealth with turmoil.*
>
> **Proverbs 15:16**

> *A good name is more desirable than great riches; to be esteemed is better than silver or gold.*
>
> **Proverbs 22:1**

> *Better the poor whose walk is blameless than the rich whose ways are perverse."*
>
> **Proverbs 28:6**

And ultimately, this is the way of Jesus. Paul lays out this example in The Christ Hymn in Philippians 2:3-4, "Do nothing out of selfish ambition or vain conceit. Rather, in humility value others above yourselves, not looking to your own interests but each of you to the interests of the others."

So, how do we actually earn all we can but not at the expense of our mind? As cliché as it sounds, pray and ask the Lord for direction. On the occasions when we've had to submit our required salary for employment, we have taken it to prayer and talked it through with each other. It's amazing how God honors the process. Remember, the end goal is not to obtain higher earnings, it's the methods you employ to get there.

Did you catch all of those? How are you doing? As you earn money, do your working patterns line up with the principles Wesley outlined?

- Are you earning all you can by honest industry, using all possible diligence in your calling?
- Are you earning all you can without paying more for it than it is worth?
- Are you earning all you can, but not at the expense of your neighbor?
- Finally, are you earning all you can, but not at the expense of your mind?

Take a minute to pause and check in with God regarding your own working habits. What, if anything, needs to change?

* * *

The people in the early days of Methodism were not affluent by any stretch. They were blue-collar workers, some employed as coal miners, who would work in horrible conditions to earn a living. Wesley believed that finance, and stewardship over those finances, were directly connected with one's spirituality, not separate from it. He encouraged those early Methodists to have a strong work ethic while increasing their own level of godliness. As these new believers started to grow in the faith, they also grew in their job responsibilities, education, and earning capacity. Wesley warned that the methods of how they earned money were now even more important to the vision they had for their financial health. We find some other great principles on earning money in Wesley's sermon, *On the Danger of Increasing Riches,* based on Psalm 62:10: "Do not trust in extortion or put vain hope in stolen goods; though your riches increase, do not set your heart on them." Let's walk through some of these principles one by one, together.

- **God is the source of our earned money.** God is the creator and sustainer of our very being. He gives us the opportunity to be employed and provide for our families and churches. Earning money is not simply contingent on our own efforts—instead God is the source of our strength and apart from Him we can't otherwise work to earn that paycheck.[9]
- **We are accountable for how we use the money we have earned.** The end goal of earning money is not simply to buy more stuff, spend frivolously on whatever we desire, or build up riches to hoard. Instead, money is a tool we use, not one that uses us. Ultimately, God is the one who holds us accountable as stewards. His hope and desire is that we exercise wisdom when it comes to money.[10]

---

[9] John Wesley, "The Sermons of John Wesley - Sermon 126 On The Danger Of Increasing Riches," The Wesley Center Online, accessed June 11, 2020, http://wesley.nnu.edu/john-wesley/the-sermons-of-john-wesley-1872-edition/sermon 126-on-the-danger-of-increasing-riches/.

[10] Ibid.

- **We are stewards of God's money.** All we have, including our very lives, does not belong to us, but to God. We should have the perspective King David had as he prayed a prayer of blessing over the gifts the Israelites offered in preparation to build the temple: "Yours, LORD, is the greatness and the power and the glory and the majesty and the splendor, for everything in heaven and earth is yours. Yours, LORD, is the kingdom; you are exalted as head over all"[11] (1 Chronicles 29:11).

- **Earning money is not just for ourselves, but to bless those in need.** Earning money isn't just about our own financial security, dreams, and desires. It goes much further than that, as Wesley points out:

  Do not you know that God entrusted you with that money (all above what buys necessities for your families) to feed the hungry, to clothe the naked, to help the stranger, the widow, the fatherless; and, indeed, as far as it will go, to relieve the wants of all mankind? How can you, how dare you, defraud your Lord, by applying it to any other purpose?[12]

  Before programs like Welfare and Medicaid, helping those in need was predominately the role of the Church and Christians working together for the common good. Are you using your money earned to bless those who have less?

---

[11] Ibid.

[12] Ibid.

- **Increasing our earnings does not give us license to waste money.** The old adage proves to be true for many Americans: "the more we earn, the more we spend." However, the question of whether money is being wasted is really determined by how we're using said money. Are we simply trying to earn more to spend on ourselves? If so, Wesley says this, "None can *afford* to throw any part of that food and raiment into the sea, which was lodged with him on purpose to feed the hungry and clothe the naked."[13] Is our striving to earn more simply to benefit ourselves, or is there a greater purpose behind it all?

While working in investment banking, Callie continued to live frugally, despite a generous salary and bonuses throughout the year. When some of her friends responded to God's call to become long-term missionaries after college, Callie was able to financially invest in their ministries. Because she was earning all she could and saving all she could, she was now in a fun position as a young working woman to be able to give all she could. Callie was already tithing to the church, but because God blessed her financially through her job in investment banking, she could also give generously to friends in missions. Callie had always found joy in giving, but now she could meet needs she had never been able to meet before.

---

[13] John Wesley, "The Sermons of John Wesley - Sermon 88 On Dress," The Wesley Center Online, accessed June 11, 2020, http://wesley.nnu.edu/john-wesley/the-sermons-of-john-wesley-1872-edition/sermon-88-on-dress/.

In his book *The Treasure Principle*, Randy Alcorn builds on what Wesley taught with a sixth and final principle on earning money: "God prospers me not to raise my standard of living, but to raise my standard of giving."[14] Alcorn based this principle on 2 Corinthians 9:11: "You will be enriched in every way so that you can be generous on every occasion..." God doesn't enrich you in every way so that you can buy everything you can get your hands on. Or so that you can hoard it all away and build bigger barns like the rich fool (Luke 12:16-21). Instead, God blesses you financially so that you can generously bless others. God could choose to give everyone the same amount of money—just enough for their needs—no more, no less. But instead, He gave us the ability to earn wealth so than we can generously bless others. There is joy in giving (more on this later), and by earning all we can and saving all we can, we have the opportunity to experience the blessing of giving.

Callie worked at her job in investment banking faithfully for two years until God called her to move back to her hometown of Lexington, KY and enter the world of charitable giving. God used those lessons from the investment banking world to prepare Callie for her next job, to give her credibility, and to teach her as she continued to work for the Lord, this time in a Christian nonprofit setting.

---

14 Alcorn, "Getting Started" in The Treasure Principle, p. 95.

While Roz was in seminary, his first job at a church was not as a youth pastor or associate pastor, but as the church custodian. It was a humbling position for him, but God taught Roz more about servanthood and the power of prayer while he was cleaning toilets and vacuuming the sanctuary than any class he took in college or seminary ever could. One of Roz's routines was to pray over the pews in the sanctuary while he was cleaning them. Roz worked as a custodian for over two years while completing his degree. Little did Roz know that a few years later he would become the senior pastor of that very church where he served as custodian when his church plant adopted that congregation. The folks at that church knew Roz's work ethic and heart, and if he cared as much about serving God through cleaning the facility, they knew how much more he would care for them as their pastor.

* * *

There is a way to work for God and not for human masters—a way to earn money without chasing it. The secret is the posture of your heart.

What matters most to you? If your bank account was empty and you had no money set aside for retirement, would you be content with God alone? Contentment is a learned skill. The apostle Paul tells the church in Philippi this:

I have learned to be content whatever the circumstances. I know what it is to be in need, and I know what it is to have plenty. I have learned the secret of being content in any and every situation, whether well fed or hungry, whether living in plenty or in want. I can do all this through [God] who gives me strength."

Philippians 4:11-13

Are you depending on God or money? What is the source of your worth, security, and contentment? It all comes down to a complete dependence on God. Money cannot buy you happiness. It cannot buy you love. It cannot buy you peace.

When it comes to earning money in a godly way, it's all about surrendering control. When we surrender all that we are and all that we have to God, money loses its hold on us. We can then work for God with all our heart, earning money without chasing it. That's when God can use the money you earn to advance the Kingdom. That's when God can use your job as ministry, whether you work for a Christian or secular organization. If God is first, God gets the glory.

What would it look like to let God's love shape your purpose where you're at right now? How could His love shape the way you work, how you raise kids or grandkids, how you interact with friends, how you act while you run errands, go to the gym, or spend time with friends? What does God's love flowing through you look like in your day-to-day life? Do you stop to listen? Are you more patient?

Do you pray for the people you see as you go about your day, whether you tell them you did or not? Do you let someone merge into traffic ahead of you, or let someone go before you in the grocery line? What could that love look like?

But remember this, your purpose in this season may look a little different than it did in the last season or even in the next. We both work full-time and have young kids, so Callie prayerfully decided that her purpose in this season has to fit within those two big containers of work and kids. But that decision did not limit her ministry. It empowered it. It gave her focus.

To retain that focus Callie asked herself questions like, "How can I let God use me more at work to love and encourage my coworkers and those we serve? How can I let God's love flow through me as I raise my kids?" Callie thought having kids would limit her ability to do ministry, but instead God has been using her kids to minister to others. Callie now has a connection point with parents and grandparents that she never had before—opening doors for conversation.

One February, our girls were handing out Valentine's Day cards at church in their sweet, little kid way. It meant so much more than if we had handed out cards—that's ministry. Or the girls will be at the grocery store or in a checkout line, and all of a sudden, they're talking to everyone within earshot! Kids don't worry what someone else might think of them, they just say "hi"— naturally opening the door for ministry to happen. Honestly, God's love flows through our girls more easily than it does us some days. Together, we're learning how God wants to use us as parents of young kids in the midst of the chaos of our everyday lives. You don't necessarily have to change careers—God may simply be calling you to change how you view your current circumstances and do ministry right where you are.

Callie learned that same lesson of living into her primary identity as a child of God by raising little girls, but actually experienced it even more fully in a different season. In 2014, when God called us to leave our home, friends, family, and life in Lexington, KY to move to Dayton, OH, Callie didn't want to go. But as God's call became clear, she took solace in the knowledge that she could continue the job she loved with National Christian Foundation Kentucky from her new home in Ohio. But God had other plans.

Instead of continuing that job remotely, God called Callie to leave that position and enter into a season of waiting on Him while doing ministry in our new church and community. Roz was the new executive pastor of new church development for Ginghamsburg United Methodist Church, and so Callie served at the church, volunteered with the local food pantry, tutored at an after-school program, worked on fixing up our new house, and built relationships with new friends in the community. Aside from some part-time contract work in financial coaching, Callie was arguably not "earning all she could" in that season. It wasn't that she didn't want to be working, but obedience to God was more important than how much money she made. All the while, God was continuing to provide for our family through Roz's work at the church.

The primary challenge Callie faced during that season was one of identity. What would others think of her? She didn't know anyone who loved to work, who could work, who didn't have kids or a family member who needed extra care, that chose not to work. Yet, God had called her to not work. Without realizing it, work had become a large part of Callie's identity. With that part of her gone, she didn't simply want to become known as "Roz's wife." Callie loved Roz, but her worth didn't need to be in her role as a wife. (For his part, Roz didn't want the pressure of being the source of Callie's worth either!) Throughout this season, God kept reminding Callie that her identity was in Him. It didn't matter what others thought of her. God's opinion was the only one that mattered. When it comes to earning all you can, it's always a matter of following God's call, even when more lucrative offers exist. Your identity as a child of God always comes first.

The main question each of us has to wrestle with money-wise is how much is enough to suit the lifestyle God is calling us to pursue? Are you engaged in the chase of money at all costs, or do you see all resources as belonging to God? Even though we're each on a different journey, how we view money matters to God.

As we've learned from our brothers and sisters recovering from addiction, we must all take inventory to help us prioritize what's most important. Take some time right now to reflect on earning money versus chasing money using this Spiritual Fruit inventory.

Spiritual Fruit Inventory: Earning vs. Chasing

If you're letting the Holy Spirit lead you in all areas of your life, including your finances, the Fruits of the Spirit outlined in Galatians 5:22-23 will be present in your life. At the end of each chapter, we invite you to do some self-reflection with a spiritual fruit inventory based on the chapter's topic.

- **Love:** Do you love God and find your worth in Him, or do you look for that worth in money?
- **Joy:** Do you find joy in serving God as you work?
- **Peace:** When you think about your income, are you anxious or at peace?
- **Patience:** Are you patient with your accumulation of wealth, or are you prone to gambling, risky investments, or other promises of shortcuts to wealth?
- **Kindness**: Remember that John Wesley says to earn all you can but not at the expense of your neighbor. Are you being kind to others in the way you earn money?
- **Goodness**: Are you doing good to your employer, employees, coworkers, and customers in the way you earn money?

- **Faithfulness:** Are you faithful to God in your work, "work[ing] at it with all your heart, as working for the Lord, not for human masters" (Colossians 3:23)?
- **Gentleness:** Wesley says to earn all you can without paying more for it than it's worth. How gentle are you in caring for your body, mind, and soul as you work? What is one change you need to make to better care for your health in this season?
- **Self-control:** Are there any areas of your work-life that feel out of control? Check for areas of workaholism, anger, sexual or emotional affairs, other relationships that cross healthy boundaries, gossip, complaining, or other sins that tend to pop up because of lack of self-control.

God, I want to honor You in all that I do. May my work be pleasing unto you. When people see me at work, may they see You. I want to be a light for your Kingdom. Search me, God, and know my heart. Test me and know my anxious thoughts. See if there is any offensive way in me, and lead me in the way everlasting (Psalm 139:23-24).

God, I confess: ________________________________.

Thank You for Your forgiveness. Help me to honor You.

In Jesus's name, Amen

CHAPTER TWO

The world's money says, "Hoard Me." God's money says, "Save Me."

Do not save what is left after spending, but spend what is left after saving.

Warren Buffet

"You need me. The more you have, the more you're worth. Protect me. Guard me. Worship me."

From a worldly perspective, this is how money talks to us. And this type of money talk doesn't just affect the wealthy. Whether you have a little or a lot, money and the greed that comes with it, can take hold of you. It can make you stingy and guarded—becoming your source of security, worth, and identity. Slowly but surely, money can become your God.

As Jesus taught His disciples:

No one can serve two masters. Either you will hate the one and love the other, or you will be devoted to the one and despise the other. You cannot serve both God and money.

Matthew 6:24

If we're not careful, money can easily replace God as our master. Someone once posed the question, "Which statement scares you more: There is no God, or there is no money in your bank account?" If you're honest with yourself, which statement raises your level of anxiety more? For many of us, running out of money is the greater fear—so we chase after it or we cling to what we do have. We hoard our money.

There are some who claim that saving isn't biblical. Jesus didn't save, so we shouldn't either, right? Jesus told the parable of the rich young ruler (Matthew 19:16-30, Mark 10:17-31, and Luke 18:18-30) in which a wealthy young man came to Jesus asking what he needed to do to earn eternal life. Jesus replied, "If you want to be perfect, go, sell your possessions and give to the poor, and you will have treasure in heaven. Then come, follow me" (Matthew 19:21). People will often argue whether this was Jesus's response to just this one individual, or if it was a command to every Christian against saving money. After all, the disciples left their livelihoods behind to follow Jesus. If we really believe in God, shouldn't we trust Him for our daily bread like the Israelites did in the wilderness? This belief system is often referred to as the "Poverty Gospel."

On the other side of things, we have this idea of the "Prosperity Gospel" preached in some churches today. The Prosperity Gospel says that if you believe in God (and give to the XYZ ministry of the person preaching), you will become richer than you ever imagined. Pretty soon you'll be driving a luxury car, living in a brand-new mansion, and going on tropical vacations every other month.

The reality of the Gospel is a little different. Scripture is filled with examples of godly men and women who were poor—whether by choice or through circumstance—such as Ruth, the widow who gave her two coins, and the story of the rich man and Lazarus.

Perhaps the most famous story of someone choosing a life of poverty for the sake of the Gospel is Jesus Himself—God becoming man to come and live on Earth as one of us. But Scripture also shows us many examples of God-fearing individuals who were wealthy and prosperous: Abraham, Joseph, King David, King Solomon, Matthew, and Lydia, just to name a few. Then there were people like Job and the apostle Paul who experienced both poverty and wealth at different points in their lives.

The question then becomes not how much money you *should* have, but how to honor God with the money you *do* have.

Saving is not something that's talked about much in church. Of course, financial gurus the world over would instruct you to build a sound savings plan in preparation for retirement. But where is the balance between being a wise saver and a hoarder? On the other end of the spectrum, we're told that our generation, and the ones after us, won't be able to retire because we've entirely neglected the principles of saving and investing.

So, where do we even start when it comes to saving money?

Spend Less than you Earn

Consider this fictional interaction based on some of the concepts found in the book *The Richest Man in Babylon:*

> There was a group of women that had all grown up together, and one day they were sitting around the table at a restaurant catching up, and they started talking about money. One woman said to the other, "I've got so much debt I don't know who to pay first. Each month I just pick a bill randomly and pay that one." Her friend said, "I know exactly what you mean. I'm worried when I get back to my apartment all my stuff is going to be on the street because we are so behind in rent." The third friend piped up and said, "I'm working as hard as I can. I got a second job just to try to cover the bills, but it doesn't ever seem to be enough." They went on for a little bit longer until one of them said, "What about Anna? How is it that she's got so much money? She grew up with us and had the same chances as us. Why is she doing so much better?"
>
> They debated it for a bit, but no one seemed to be able to figure out why, so they decided to track down their friend Anna. They called her up and convinced her to come join them. "Anna," they said, "How is that you have so much money? You grew up with us. Did you win the lottery or something? Did you have a rich great uncle that died and left you everything? Did you find yourself a sugar daddy?" Anna laughed. "No, no and no," she said. They would not let her off the hook that easily. "What's your secret then?" they said. "You've got to share with us."
>
> Anna leaned forward and so did her friends who looked at her expectantly. "You've got to pay yourself *first."* They looked at her like she was crazy, and one of them said, "What are you talking about? All the money we make gets paid

to us, except what they take out in taxes." "Yes," she said, "but then you go to the store and pay them for a new pair of jeans, you pay the grocery for food and snacks, you pay your landlord for rent. At the end of the day, you don't have anything left for yourself. You've got to pay yourself first. I started out in the same financial position you were, except I met this lady a long time ago who told me to pay myself first. So, every time I got paid, I started taking $1 out of every $10 and putting it aside. I wouldn't spend it. And slowly $1 became $10 and $10 became $100 and $100 became $1,000. And you get the idea." The friends liked this. They tried to talk Anna into sharing some of her money with them, but she told them no way. Not because she did not want to share with them, but because she explained to them the sense of accomplishment they would feel once they had saved that much on their own was worth more than the money itself.[15]

The first step to getting your finances in order is to spend less than you make. Easier said than done. You have to pay yourself first, then you have to make a plan to stretch the rest of your money to cover your expenses. It's so easy for spending to get out of hand. The question is, do you want your money to control you, or do you want to control your money?

If you want to control your money, you must make a spending plan, a budget. More on that in the next chapter, but part of that budget is setting aside a percentage of your income to go toward giving first and saving second before you spend another dollar. In essence, you're giving to God first and paying yourself second.

---

15 George S. Clason, *The Richest Man in Babylon* (CreateSpace Independent Publishing Platform; Anniversary Edition, 2014).

Build Liquidity

Building liquidity is what starts to happen when you spend less than you earn—your money begins to accumulate. "Liquidity" is a fancy financial term that simply means having enough cash (or funds that can easily convert to cash) to cover short-term expenses and debt payments. Many call this an emergency fund. It's money on hand that you do not use unless an emergency comes up—for example, your car or home needs a repair, or you get sick and have to take a short-term, unpaid leave from work. Liquidity gives you a cushion, and it keeps you from having to put those emergencies on a credit card that charges high interest until you can pay it off.

Set a goal for that emergency fund. An emergency fund of $1,000 is a great place to start if you don't have any savings right now. Some of you might be good savers and $1,000 doesn't sound too hard. For others, that's a big goal. Break it down and start with a goal of $100, then $300, then $500, then $800, then $1,000. Break goals into smaller chunks, and set reasonable expectations.

You eventually want to get about three-to-six months of living expenses in your emergency fund. The number of months you need varies based on the uncertainty of your job field, your personal health, and whether you have other income sources. For instance, a household with both spouses working and income from a side job or two might be completely comfortable with three months of living expenses saved. If one person lost their job, they could reduce expenses and live off the other person's salary for a while during a job search. On the other hand, a single-income household with multiple people to provide for in an uncertain job market would want closer to a six-month cushion. Start small and work your way there.

What happens if you need to tap into your emergency fund? That's okay. That's what it's there for. Just make sure this is truly an emergency and not something like a vacation to Disney World. When you need to use your emergency fund, replenish it as extra income starts to come in. Continue to pay yourself first, and it will start to accumulate once again.

Save for Long-Term Purchases

Once you have a minimum of $1,000 in an emergency fund, do not stop saving. Keep paying yourself first to grow that emergency fund and to save for long-term purchases: a car, a down payment on a home, a wedding, a vacation, college, retirement, etc.

While saving from your regular income is a wise consistent practice, you can speed up your progress on savings goals by setting aside money from tax returns, any cash gifts you receive, or other sources of spontaneous income. Maybe you take some additional odd jobs, pick up a few extra shifts at work, or get crafty and sell some of your creations—all with the intent of using that extra income to accelerate your savings progress or other financial goals. When you're intentional and work a plan, you'll be surprised how slowly but surely you make incredible progress.

Don't get discouraged. Proverbs 21:5 reminds us, "Steady plodding brings prosperity, but hasty speculation brings poverty" (The Living Bible). Do not get distracted by get-rich-quick schemes. If it sounds too good to be true, it probably is. When you're faithful over the long-term, your future will be prosperous.

However, if you can accomplish all three steps above, what's next? How much is enough?

Money says, "There is never enough. You need me to be happy. You need more to sleep easy." God, on the other hand, says, "'Come to me all who are weary and you will find rest. Take my yoke upon you and learn from me for I am gentle and humble in heart and you will find rest for your soul' (Matthew 11:28-30). Trust Me to provide. I am your source of joy and contentment."

Like Paul, we must learn to be content in both seasons of plenty and seasons of want. (Philippians 4:11-13). There's a secret here. If you learn it, you will find joy and happiness all the days of your life. If you don't, like Solomon, you will find yourself lamenting meaningless toil and wealth accumulation as chasing after the wind:

> *So I hated life, because the work that is done under the sun was grievous to me. All of it is meaningless, a chasing after the wind. I hated all the things I had toiled for under the*

sun, because I must leave them to the one who comes after me. And who knows whether that person will be wise or foolish? Yet they will have control over all the fruit of my toil into which I have poured my effort and skill under the sun. This too is meaningless.

Ecclesiastes 2:17-19

Ultimately, money doesn't come with us into eternity. You will eventually have to leave it to someone who comes after you, and at that point you have no control over what they do with it.

Even while we're alive, money can be here one day and gone the next. In His Sermon on the Mount, Jesus warns against trying to store up riches here on Earth:

Do not store up for yourselves treasures on earth, where moths and vermin destroy, and where thieves break in and steal. But store up for yourselves treasures in heaven, where moths and vermin do not destroy, and where thieves do not break in and steal.

Matthew 6:19-20

Few earthly possessions are long-lasting, and none are eternal. It's what you do with your money that counts. So why save?

James 5:1-3 says, "Now listen, you rich people, weep and wail because of the misery that is coming on you. Your wealth has rotted, and moths have eaten your clothes. Your gold and silver are corroded. Their corrosion will testify against you and eat your flesh like fire. You have hoarded wealth in the last days."

James isn't saying that saving is a terrible thing to do, but when we hoard money simply for ourselves it will not last. John Wesley understood that saving has to be done with a purpose in mind—avoiding any unnecessary expenses that are wasteful. In other words, purchase what you need but don't be extravagant, keep it basic. It all comes down to living a life of simplicity by deciding what we require and what we're willing to go without.

Wesley also laid out a few cautions about saving:

- "Do not waste your resources on trivial expenses, which is the same as throwing your money into the ocean."
- "Do not waste any of your precious resources merely in gratifying the desires of the flesh."
- "Do not waste any part of your valuable resources gratifying the desire of the eye with extravagant or expensive clothing or needless accessories."
- "Spend no money to gratify the pride of life or to gain the admiration and praise of others."[16]

When speaking on saving all you can, one of Wesley's most quoted Scripture passages was the parable of the talents in Matthew 25 and Luke 16:9: "I tell you, use worldly wealth to gain friends for yourselves, so that when it is gone, you will be welcomed into eternal dwellings." Wesley makes six different references to "talents" in his

[16] John Wesley. "John Wesley on the Use of Money: By Observing Three Simple Rules, We Can Become Faithful Managers of Money," Enrichment Journal, accessed February 21, 2021, https://enrichmentjournal.ag.org/Issues/2015/Winter-2015/John-Wesley-on-the-Use-of-Money.

sermon *The Use of Money*. When it comes to money, the key is remembering that everything belongs to God. Human beings are simply stewarding the resources God has given us. Like Wesley, this parable distinguishes saving from hoarding. The two servants who saved wisely and put their master's money to work were rewarded greatly. The master repeated his praise for both of them saying, "Well done, good and faithful servant! You have been faithful with a few things; I will put you in charge of many things. Come and share your master's happiness!"

But one servant came back and reported that he took the talent he had been given and hid it in the ground. In his viewpoint, that servant thought he was doing the master a favor by saving his talent. In reality he was hoarding. There was no end goal for the buried money— it didn't serve a purpose. The servant was surprised to hear his master say, "You wicked, lazy servant! So you knew that I harvest where I have not sown and gather where I have not scattered seed? Well then, you should have put my money on deposit with the bankers, so that when I returned I would have received it back with interest. So take the bag of gold from him and give it to the one who has ten bags."

You might think the servant's actions in this situation were silly and reckless, but not that long ago, with distrust of financial institutions at an all-time high, people started to hoard cash, something that's still not uncommon today. Here are some real-life examples:

- $11 million worth of gold coins were found in a backyard.
- $200,000 worth of coins were hidden in the wall of an abandoned house.
- A $27,630 rare painting was found in a thrift store couch that cost a mere $215.
- $182,000 was found inside a bathroom wall dating back to the Great Depression.
- $426,856 worth of ancient coins were found in a farmer's field of barley in Britain.
- One of twenty-four original copies of the Declaration of Independence was found in a $4 framed painting that was auctioned for $8.14 million in 1999.
- $500,000 worth of coins were found in an auction storage unit that sold for $1,100.[17]

It's undeniable, the human heart wants to hoard what we've been given—to bury it or hide it away and never let it see the light of day again unless someone take away what we've worked so hard to "earn."

While we're on the topic of hoarding, let's look at some of the other wise principles Wesley shares in his sermon *The Use of Money*:

- "Having gained all you can, by honest wisdom and unwearied diligence, the second rule of Christian prudence is, 'Save all you can'..."

---

17 Kyli Singh, "7 Times People Found Money in Bizarre Places," Mashable (Mashable, September 10, 2014), last modified September 10, 2014, accessed April 1, 2021, https://mashable.com/2014/09/10/hidden-treasure-weird-places/.

- "Do not waste any part of so precious a talent merely in gratifying the desires of the flesh; in procuring the pleasures of sense of whatever kind; particularly, in enlarging the pleasure of tasting…"

- "Do not waste any part of so precious a talent merely in gratifying the desire of the eye by superfluous or expensive apparel, or by needless ornaments. Waste no part of it in curiously adorning your houses; in superfluous or expensive furniture; in costly pictures, painting, gilding, books; in elegant rather than useful gardens…"

- "Lay out nothing to gratify the pride of life, to gain the admiration or praise of men. This motive of expense is frequently interwoven with one or both of the former…"

- "If I had one child, elder or younger, who knew the value of money; one who I believed, would put it to the true use, I should think it my absolute, indispensable duty to leave that child the bulk of my fortune; and to the rest just so much as would enable them to live in the manner they had been accustomed to do." But what, if all your children were equally ignorant of the true use of money? "I should then give each what would keep him above want, and to bestow all the rest in such a manner as I judged would be most for the glory of God."[18]

Let's linger on this last point for a minute. In the Bible, the children of Israel were not all treated equally. When they entered the promised land, the descendants of Levi

[18] John Wesley, "Use of Money," Christian History Institute, accessed December 4, 2020, https://christianhistoryinstitute.org/magazine/article/wesleys-sermon-use-of-money.

weren't given land as an inheritance like the other tribes of Israel. But this was not a punishment. On the contrary, it was a greater blessing. As A.W. Tozer explains:

> *God said to him simply, 'I am thy part and thine inheritance,' and by those simple words made him richer than all his brethren, richer than all the kings and rajas who have ever lived in the world... The man who has God for his treasure has all things in One.* [19]

When God is your source, your ultimate inheritance, the stock market can crash, you can go bankrupt through no fault of your own, but your true worth, your eternal inheritance, never moves. You can be the richest person in the world's eyes or the poorest individual that's ever walked the Earth, and because you're a child of God you already have all you could ever need.

In saving and planning for the future we hold this tension, knowing Heaven, not Earth, is our home. We don't know the number of our days and even our best laid plans can come to ruin, but the one thing we do know—the one thing that is certain—is that Jesus is Lord, and when we accept him as our Lord and Savior everything changes. God's perfect love casts out fear (1 John 4:18). God's peace that surpasses all understanding washes away anxious thoughts (Philippians 4:6-7). God will keep the person in perfect peace whose mind is fixed on Him because that

---

[19] A. W. Tozer, *Three Spiritual Classics in One Volume: The Knowledge of the Holy, The Pursuit of God, and God's Pursuit of Man.* (Chicago, IL: Moody Publishers, 2018), p. 227.

person trusts in God (Isaiah 26:3). Where is your hope? Where is your peace? Where is your trust?

Freedom comes in surrendering all that we have and all that we are to the Lord. Surrender is the single most powerful tool to achieving financial freedom. A financial advisor may promise freedom if you allow him or her to invest your money, but even the savviest investor can't guarantee peace of mind—only God can do that.

Surrender is an ongoing process. It's a letting go of control. It's not negligence. It's putting your full trust in the Lord of lords and King of kings. Each time you feel the temptation to hoard or to worry about money, name those feelings. Tell God exactly how you're feeling and then surrender the sources of those feelings to Him: your expenses, your investments, your home, your car, your appliance that stopped working, your retirement, your debt, your checking and savings accounts—whatever it is that's clamoring for your worship or worry. What you worry about is often what you're worshiping. Stop and surrender. God knows exactly what you're feeling. He knows your situation and the outcome of that situation better than you can know it yourself. Stop and surrender. Stop and surrender again and again each time those feelings emerge.

A powerful practice of surrender Roz and I do ourselves begins by closing your eyes and placing your hands palms up in your lap. Visualize all that you are carrying, all the worries and fears and concerns in your hands. See each one, and mentally place them in your hands. Then, imagine God's big, all-powerful, loving hands are under your own. Take a deep breath and slowly turn your hands over, placing all of those things into God's hands. Simply saying to Him, *Lord, into Your hands I surrender all these things. I love You. I trust You. I need more of You in my life. Please fill me up with You instead.*

Turn your hands palms up again, and imagine receiving all the good things God has promised you: His love, joy, peace, patience, kindness, goodness, faithfulness, gentleness, and self-control, His grace and forgiveness, the gift of His own Son, an eternal inheritance that cannot be shaken, His presence with you here on Earth, all the many blessings He has given you to enjoy here and now—receive each one with a prayer of gratitude: *God, thank You. You have blessed me abundantly more than I deserve. Thank You for loving me.*

* * *

So, how do you know if you're hoarding what you've been given? Starting with possessions is often easier than objectively looking at your bank account. First, take a look at your stuff. Do you have more than you need right now? What would it look like to go through your home, starting with just one room, and get rid of everything you no longer use? Are you worried you might one day need something you get rid of? Are you worried about running out and not having enough? We complain about clutter, but very rarely do we actually do anything to eliminate the mess. Sell what you can sell. Donate what you can donate. If you've never used an item before, chances are you never will.

While you're at it, where do you need to declutter spiritually? What hurt, bitterness, or soul wounds are you holding onto? Invite God in. Forgiveness can be a powerful tool for letting go. Let God free you up, not just physically, but spiritually, mentally, and emotionally as well. Callie's mom had a prayer book as a teenager that she passed onto Callie. In the inside of the front cover, she had written the simple words: "Let Go. Let God." Where do you need to let go, and let God have control? Make room in your heart and home.

Finally, take a look at your bank account, look at your investments and any retirement savings you have and prayerfully ask God if you're saving wisely, neglecting your savings, or hoarding. It all boils down to the question: How much is enough? The answer to that question will be different for each person based on the cost of living in your area, your lifestyle, life expectancy, health, etc., but you can estimate a number.

Roz and I have always loved giving, to the point where we worried we might not be saving enough to retire one day. But we were just speculating. We'd never actually checked how much we were saving or run any rough numbers. So, we asked our financial advisor if he could do some projections for us. We gave him a couple scenarios of retirement ages and used current income, spending, and saving levels to project what we would need in future dollars based on inflation. It turned out that we were right about where we needed to be, which gave us peace of mind as we continued to give generously, spend responsibly, and save for the future.

Most financial firms can run these types of numbers for you. If you have retirement accounts, a great place to start is with the financial firm that holds your accounts. There are also online tools, but it's often helpful to have a professional look at the numbers with you. They might tell you that you're behind in your saving if you didn't start planning for retirement until later in life or you didn't make it a priority. Don't fret. Instead, pray about it, surrender your finances to the Lord, and start now. Work through the steps we outlined earlier to start paying yourself first, build liquidity, and save for the future.

Maybe you're already in retirement and you're worried you will outlive your savings. This is a great conversation to have with your financial advisor as well. He or she can help you look at several different scenarios and you can make lifestyle adjustments now, if needed.

The truth is, if you never figure out how much is enough to live on—if you never determine that financial finish line—you will undoubtedly be tempted to hoard if you're a saver or overspend if you're a spender. Either way, you will be plagued with worry and anxiety anytime the topic of money comes up. Not talking about your money goals can create incredible tension in a marriage too, especially if you're wired in different ways and one of you wants to save while the other keeps buying. When you have a number to work toward, you can make a plan to get there, together. That number allows you to continue giving generously now, and even more generously when you reach your goal. There is freedom in knowing.

Still, this topic can create anxiety for many. When this is the case, go back to God's Word. The apostle Paul wasn't kidding when he said, "Do not be anxious about anything, but in every situation, by prayer and petition, with thanksgiving, present your requests to God. And the peace of God, which transcends all understanding, will guard your hearts and your minds in Christ Jesus" (Philippians 4:6-7). Pray about your finances. That is not selfish—it's wise. Praying about finances isn't trivial. Instead, it can help grow your trust in God.

The key in every area of your finances is putting God first. When you do, watch how He provides. The Israelites spent 40 years in the wilderness totally dependent on God. He provided manna each morning: a white flakey substance like bread. Manna literally means "What is it?" in Hebrew. Each morning, the Israelites were told to gather what they needed for that one day. This rule was to protect them from hoarding—if they gathered more than they needed, the manna became infested with maggots. There was one exception. The day before the Sabbath, the Israelites were to gather twice as much manna so they could rest on the Sabbath, and for that day— that one extra day—it would not rot (Exodus 16). God was teaching them trust. Where in your own life is God teaching you to trust Him? This isn't a Poverty Gospel, nor is it a Prosperity Gospel. Instead, saving is all about having a heart that's right before God—a heart that trusts Him enough to say, *I am not going to hoard money or things because God alone is my portion.*

This is not to say that we shouldn't save. Through Joseph, God instructed the Egyptians to save during the seven years of plenty to prepare for the seven years of famine that would follow. Pharaoh trusted Joseph, and Joseph kept all of Egypt, and ultimately his own family and the Israelite people, from starving (Genesis 41-47). Joseph trusted God enough to save when God said to save.

The difference between Joseph and the Israelites trying to hoard manna was the posture of their hearts. When God said save, Joseph saved. When God told the Israelites not to hoard, they had to trust and only gather enough for the day ahead. God will lead and guide you if you let Him, and that applies as much to money as it does every other area of your life.

Let God be your provider. If you need a reminder, look at a dollar bill. Find those words that say, "In God we trust." There is a visible reminder of God's provision on the very wealth in your wallet. As the Israelites prepared to enter the promised land, Moses reminded them of how God provided manna in the wilderness, how God kept even their clothes from wearing out. Moses cautioned them:

> *[God] gave you manna to eat in the wilderness, something your ancestors had never known, to humble and test you so that in the end it might go well with you. You may say to yourself, 'My power and the strength of my hands have produced this wealth for me.' But remember the Lord your God, for it is he who gives you the ability to produce wealth...*
>
> **Deuteronomy 8:16-18.**

Who gave you the wealth you have? Even if you didn't inherit a dime from your family and worked hard to build wealth up yourself, God gave you the strength of your hands and the creativity of your mind. God is the One who gave you the very ability to build the wealth you have, whether that's a lot or a little. Give God thanks for all you have.

What if you don't have much? Still give thanks to God for all you have. God has blessed you. As you give thanks and recognize the source of what you have, gratitude becomes a heart-changer. Gratitude recognizes God as your provider, your source, your sustainer. Gratitude moves your mentality from one of hoarding to one of saving—from trusting in yourself to trusting in God. What you have materially could be gone tomorrow, but God promises never to leave you nor forsake you (Joshua 1:9). As long as you have God, you have more than enough.

This quote has been circulating on social media recently:

> *The pessimist sees the glass as half-empty. The optimist sees the glass as half-full. The psalmist says: My cup runneth over.*

As women and men of faith, we believe that we have a God who came that we might have life abundant (John 10:10).

When Callie was younger, she wanted to be a middle school math teacher. She always loved numbers, equations, and graphs. As she got older, Callie realized how challenging the classroom management side of teaching is. (If you're a teacher, God bless you!) So instead of going into education, Callie took her love for numbers and entered the world of finance and ultimately, charitable giving. In this field, she discovered there were people hungry to learn about finances and how to encourage generosity. This has given her the opportunity to teach without (as many!) of the classroom management challenges involved.

Even though she never ended up being a teacher, one thing Callie never lost from that time was her love for a good chart or graph. So, whether you're a math person or not, we hope you will indulge us as we use a graph to help identify where we as individuals are and where we want to be when it comes to spiritual and financial wealth.

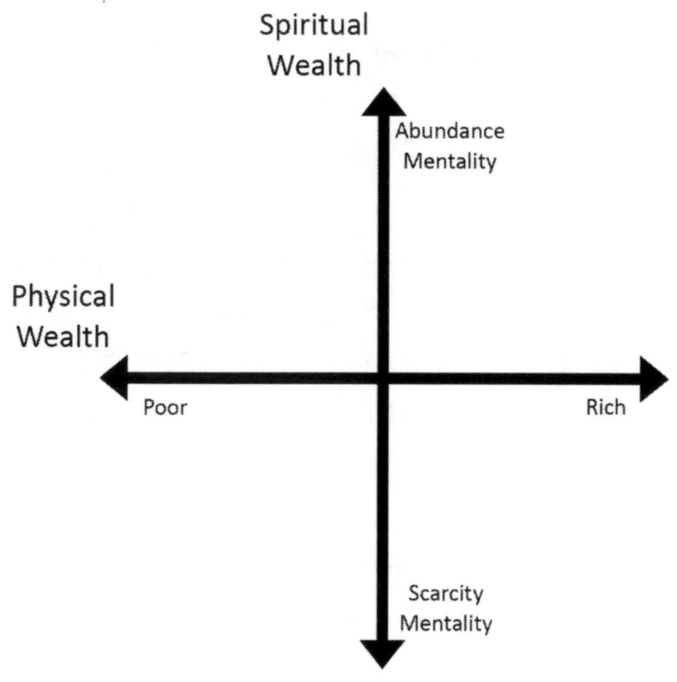

The graph above indicates, when it comes to financial and spiritual wealth, there are four categories of churches and individuals. Each is represented by one of the four quadrants of the graph. On the horizontal axis (the x-axis if you remember from your middle school math days), is financial wealth. There are churches and individuals that are financially rich, and then there are those that are financially poor.

It's generally pretty easy to figure out where individuals and churches stand with financial wealth. Look at the people and churches around you. Though the tendency is to compare ourselves to those who have more than us and downplay our own wealth, take an honest assessment and see what you find.

One of the best sermons on wealth we've heard is from Pastor Andy Stanley's *How to be Rich* series. The first sermon in the series is called "Congratulations." It can be found through North Point Resources if you want to listen to it.[20] In this sermon, Pastor Stanley talks about "those rich people" who are so wealthy they have an extra house just for their car. They call it a garage. These people have so much food in their house that they have to throw old food away to make room for the new food. They have so many toys for their kids that they run out of room. They have so much money that they rip out working counters in their kitchen to replace them with new counters, and then they have to live with the mess that they created. It's very hard being rich. The rich people look at a closet full of clothes and say, "I have nothing to wear." They take perfectly good cars and go through the hassle of selling them and buying new ones, when the one they had still functioned. They get paid for not coming to work because they have so much vacation time, and then they have to go through the hassle of planning what to do with that extra time. There is so much extra

---

[20] Andy Stanley, "How To Be Rich, Part 1 - Congratulations," North Point Resources, accessed September 25, 2020, https://store.northpoint.org/products/how-to-be-rich-part-1-congratulations.

complexity to being rich. Of course, Pastor Stanley is saying all of this tongue-in-cheek. We're much too quick to compare ourselves to those who have more than we do, so therefore we don't often *feel* rich. But the reality is, many of us actually are.

There is a great tool called "How Rich Am I?" on givingwhatwecan.org. The Giving What We Can website encourages gifts to certain non-profits that we don't necessarily endorse, but the calculator on their website allows you to calculate how rich you are compared to the rest of the world's population. Then it lets you explore your standing if you were to give a percentage of your income away. Here are some examples:

- A family of two adults and five children in the United States with a post-tax income of $80,000 would be in the richest 10.1% of the global population.
- A family of one adult and two children in the United States with a post-tax income of $45,000 would be in the richest 7.9% of the global population.
- A single adult in the United States with a post-tax income of $40,000 would be in the richest 2.6% of the global population.
- A family of two adults and one child in the United States with a post-tax income of $120,000 would be in the richest 1.2% of the global population.[21]

---

[21] Giving What We Can, "How Rich Am I?," accessed February 14, 2021, https://howrichami.givingwhatwecan.org/how-rich-am-i.

If you're reading this book, chances are you're rich. You might not feel like it, but you have an abundance of financial resources that the majority of people don't have.

Next, let's look at the vertical axis of the graph (the y-axis): spiritual wealth. Spiritual wealth is so much more important than physical wealth. There are churches and individuals that live with an abundance mentality and those that live with a scarcity mentality whether they're financially wealthy or not. The terms "abundance mentality" and "scarcity mentality" were coined by Stephen Covey in his book *The 7 Habits of Highly Effective People.* He writes:

> *"Most people are deeply scripted in what I call the Scarcity Mentality. They see life as having only so much, as though there were only one pie out there. And if someone were to get a big piece of the pie, it would mean less for everybody else. The Scarcity Mentality is the zero-sum paradigm of life. People with a Scarcity Mentality have a very difficult time sharing recognition and credit, power or profit..."* [22]

If someone is living with a scarcity mentality, then regardless of how much financial wealth this church or individual has, there is never going to be enough, or there's a strong fear of losing what does exist. The scarcity mentality desires to hold onto things tightly. Here are some examples of what a scarcity mentality might sound like in relation to things like money, time and people:

---

[22] Stephen R. Covey, "Habit 4: Think Win/Win," in *The 7 Habits of Highly Effective People* (New York, NY: Simon and Schuster, 2004), p. 219.

- **Money** – "The budget for ministry may be $0, but at least the utility bills are paid and the building hasn't fallen down." For an individual with a scarcity mentality, regardless of the size of their paycheck, they are afraid to give any of it away. "What if there's not enough for tomorrow?" "Will that person do with my money what they said they will?" This person may resemble Ebenezer Scrooge in *A Christmas Carol* before he was visited by the ghosts of Christmas past, present, and future.

- **Physical Space** – "What if an outside group comes in and makes a mess?" "Youth want to come into our church? They'll wreck the place!" "My house is my house. I worked for it and bought it with my hard-earned money."

- **Time** – "If I serve, then I won't have time for all of my normal activities … the shows I watch, parties, video games, working out, etc." "If I serve once, they're going to expect me to do it all the time, so I won't serve at all. Eventually, they'll just stop asking." People probably won't say it exactly that way, but that's often the underlying point. Instead, most will simply say, "I don't have time. I'm too busy." Some people truly are too busy, but we typically make time for what we want to make time for.

- **People** – "If we partner on an event with another church or organization, who gets the credit for the people that show up? Our own people may choose to go to that church instead." Individuals with a scarcity mentality may get upset with friends who get married, have kids, move to another city, etc. because it changes the dynamics of their friendship. They have a hard time being excited for that friend or loved one because they're focused primarily on what they will be losing.

- **The Past** – "When I started coming to this church it was standing-room only and the nursery was overflowing." That kind of statement is often made while standing in a church that's nearly empty, but rather than change their behavior, the members with a scarcity mentality want to live in the memory of past glory days. "When I was a kid, they always told me I'd be a doctor." Or on the flip side, "My parents always told me I'd never amount to anything." Those statements can often become self-fulfilling prophecies despite changes in interest and personal growth. We can learn from the past, but if we dwell there it's hard to move into the future. Some individuals hold so firmly to the past that they're completely unwilling to try new things, this pattern of behavior comes out even more around the holidays when traditions take center stage. It's like the Israelites who wanted to go back to the slavery of Egypt rather than enter the land God had promised for them.

- **The Status Quo** – "This is how we have always done things." "My grandma made that with her own hands for the church 85 years ago. How dare you even think of taking it down!" "If you stop that ministry, you know a lot of people will leave." That ministry might have been thriving in the past and is no longer effective today, but because there has always been a _________ ministry, these scarcity mentality individuals cannot imagine church without it. This individual may be stuck in an unhealthy relationship, a job they can't stand, or a lifestyle of overeating or addiction, but they fear change so much that they stay in that unhealthy status quo.

- Power – The same matriarch or patriarch has run things for so long that they refuse to give up that role. If you challenge them, they'll run you out of the church. This individual keeps others around them from growing or advancing because it might mean that they wouldn't be able to control them anymore. Every person with talent or ability is a threat because if they share their power with that person, the scarcity mentality person might lose it completely.

Those churches and individuals living with a scarcity mentality focus on themselves first— fearful they might not have enough. They look at how much money is in the bank account rather than how big their God is. That fear causes them to hold what they do have tightly.

Fortunately, at the other end of the spectrum is the abundance mentality. Covey describes it this way:

> *The Abundance Mentality, on the other hand, flows out of a deep inner sense of personal worth and security. It is the paradigm that there is plenty out there and enough to spare for everybody. It results in sharing of prestige, of recognition, of profits, of decision making. It opens possibilities, options, alternatives, and creativity.*[23]

This describes how all Christians should be if we are walking with Jesus Christ. This is exactly the mindset Jesus modeled:

---

[23] Stephen R. Covey, "Habit 4: Think Win/Win," in *The 7 Habits of Highly Effective People* (New York, NY: Simon and Schuster, 2004), p. 220.

For the Son of Man came not to be served but to serve, and to give his life a ransom for many.

Mark 10:45

After he had washed their feet, had put on his robe, and had returned to the table, he said to them, "Do you know what I have done to you? You call me Teacher and Lord—and you are right, for that is what I am. So if I, your Lord and Teacher, have washed your feet, you also ought to wash one another's feet."

John 13:12-14

[Jesus] emptied himself, taking the form of a slave, being born in human likeness. And being found in human form, he humbled himself and became obedient to the point of death—even death on a cross.

Philippians 2:7-8)

We follow a God who gave it all up: power, prestige, wealth, time, His home, and ultimately His life. But death is not the end. This life on Earth is not our final destination. So why hoard and store up treasures on Earth "where moth and rust consume and where thieves break in and steal" when we can instead store up treasure in Heaven (Matthew 6:21)?

Jesus taught the counter-cultural power of an abundance mindset, realizing that in giving the things of this life away, we actually gain so much more. He explained it this way, "If any want to become my followers, let them deny themselves and take up their cross daily and follow me. For those who want to save their life will lose it, and those who lose their life for my sake will save it" (Luke 9:23-24).

Jesus washed the feet of his disciples and God calls us to

do the same. When we give away the resources, power, and prestige we do have, God's Kingdom can advance, and we end up gaining more than we ever thought we would lose.

Those with an abundance mentality are living out of faith, not fear—their focus on the Lord and on His abundance and goodness. These individuals are generous and willing to share of their resources. They also understand that God owns it all—they're simply in charge of managing those resources they have been entrusted with.

Now, wherever you are financially on the graph, hopefully you're living spiritually with an abundance mentality. The good news is when we surrender all we have and all we are to God, the Lord meets us there and helps us grow. So take a look at this graph again, and see if you can honestly mark where you are today.

Are you living with an abundance mentality? Are you trusting God and living generously, faithfully using the time, talent, and financial resources the Lord has entrusted into your care for the building up of the Kingdom? Are you listening to God and being obedient? When was the last time you took a risk that you felt the Lord was leading you to take? How much of your possessions could you or would you be willing to give away if the Lord prompted you? Jesus challenged the rich young ruler in Matthew 19:21, "If you wish to be perfect, go, sell your possessions, and give the money to the poor, and you will have treasure in heaven; then come, follow me." If Jesus made a similar request of you, how would you respond?

God does not call everyone to sell everything to follow Him, but He never tells anyone in Scripture to hoard it all here on Earth and be stingy. Most of us wouldn't describe ourselves as stingy, but when you look at your giving and the way you share or guard your time, how would someone on the outside describe you?

Regardless of where you are, start with an honest assessment of yourself.

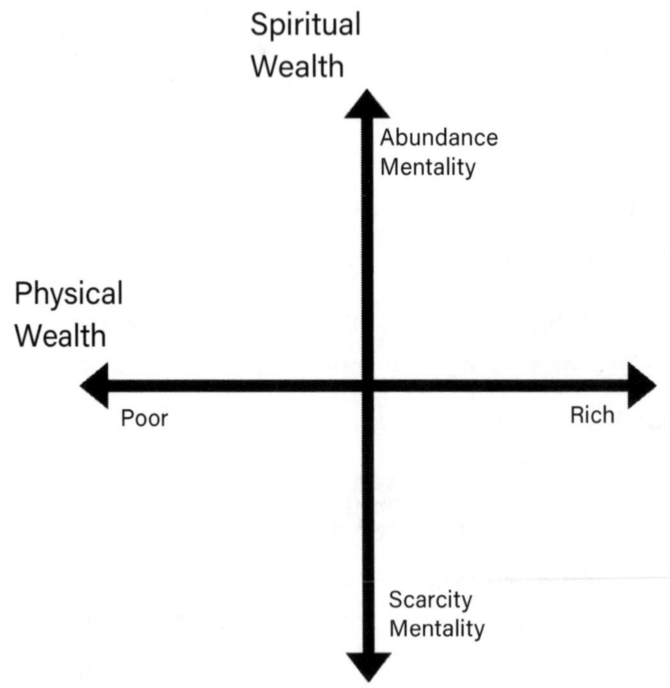

Once you've marked where you are today, next mark where you would like to be, and start praying (and continue reading) about how to get there.

One of the key ways to move to an abundance mentality and be able to save without hoarding is through surrender. In the spring 2010, Roz proposed to Callie. Callie said "Yes" but under one condition: Roz had to go through the Crown Financial Ministries Biblical Financial Study with her. She wanted them to be on same page about how they managed God's money. Yes, we just called it "God's money." One of the key principles of the Crown Financial Ministries study is that God is the owner of our money and our role is that of managers. Instead of referring to *my* money, *my* house, *my* car, etc., even shifting our language became key as we went through the course. We started referring to things with the definite article, calling them *the* bank account, *the* house, *the* car, etc. Some people go so far as to call them *God's* money, *God's* house, and *God's* car. The study invites you to fill out a Quit Claim Deed naming the things that you are transferring out of your ownership and into God's. Now, the document is not binding in any legal systems of this world, but it is a powerful action spiritually to surrender control of all that you have to the Lord.[24]

What would it look like for you to surrender control of your stuff to God? If something belongs to God, how do you care for it? With more attention? If it belongs to God and God told you to give it away or sell it, would you be more open? If something happens to a possession, would you

[24] *Crown Biblical Financial Study: Life Group Manual* (Knoxville, TN: Crown Financial Ministries, 2013).

respond with more trust knowing that God is able to give and take away?

It's hard to surrender. There is almost an internal feeling of needing to "protect" that possession, that loved one. If we surrender, what will God do? What might God ask us to give up? Back up and remember Who you are surrendering those things to: your Creator, your Loving Father, the One who gave everything to you from the beginning. We think we're protecting our things when we hold back, but really we're hindering and blocking God's provision. When we surrender, God is free to move in miraculous ways, to really use you and move through you to bless others, and in the process, you yourself will be blessed.

Fear is the biggest opponent to faith, especially in the area of finances. Fear says you won't have enough. You need more. The antidote to fear is a deep level of trust. It's surrendering control of all that you have to God and making the conscious choice to walk by faith instead. This doesn't mean being foolish, though it might look that way sometimes in the world's eyes. Instead, it's seeking God for wisdom in the area of your finances—what to give, when to invest, when to buy, and when to wait on God's perfect timing. There are other times where God will say to wait when it feels like everyone is buying the latest invention. Trust God's timing. Then, there are times where everyone else wants to wait and God calls you to lead with a gift, an investment, or a risk that doesn't make sense in the world's eyes. How is God calling you to live by faith?

If it all belongs to God, how you spend your money and invest it becomes a lot more important. We will talk more about spending in the next chapter, but let's talk for a minute right now about investing.

How would God want you to invest His money? There are seemingly endless investment choices, but some will align with your faith more than others. Biblically Responsible Investing (BRI) has become more and more popular with its goal of aligning investments with biblical values. BRI screens for things like human rights abuses, drugs and alcohol, pornography, and gambling, excluding companies that engage in those activities. When possible, they choose to support those companies with a Christian business model—companies that value employees, give back to the community generously, produce products that help people, strengthen families, and honor God.

Many of these investment funds also use their rights as a shareholder to encourage companies to act in a way that honors God. Wespath, for example, manages the retirement funds for the United Methodist Church. This company has chosen to take on climate change as one of its core issues out of care and concern for God's creation. Wespath uses the size of their assets and portfolio to encourage some of the companies contributing the most to global emissions to diversify into sustainable energy. They also engage companies on issues related to climate change and board diversity.[25] Wespath is just one example of an investment company that is working on incorporating biblical principles into the way they invest money.

When investing God's money, the other area to consider is risk versus return. Risk is the likelihood of sustaining large losses often because of a desire to get rich quickly. Return is how much the money earns through a given investment. Usually, the greater the risk a person is willing to take, the greater the possible returns, and conversely, the greater the potential loss. The lower the risk, the lower the possible returns. It's a balance.

Let's consider again the parable of the bags of gold, or the parable of the ten talents (Matthew 25:14-30), this time looking at it from an investing perspective. In the parable, a master goes away and entrusts his money to three servants. To one, he gives five bags of gold, to another two bags, and to the third one bag. The first two servants invest their master's money and double it. The third dug a hole and buried the one bag he had. When the master returned, the first two servants were praised for their wise management of their master's money and given more to manage as a result. The third servant was chastised and kicked out for not taking any risk at all and earning zero return on what the master had entrusted into his care.

---

[25] "Shareholder Engagement," Wespath Benefits | Investments, accessed September 25, 2020, https://www.wespath.org/retirement-investments/investment-information/investment-philosophy/sustainable-investment/Shareholder-Engagement.

While this parable can have many applications to the Kingdom of God (like we saw with saving before), the surface level money application here should not be lost. The story clearly ties to the truth of God as the owner and we as the managers of His money. We see two servants, or managers, who invest the money wisely, earning a good return. The third servant doesn't take any risk at all. He buries the money. Often, we are so attached to our money that we're afraid to part with any of it. That is also a form of hoarding. If it's God's money, there is an appropriate level of risk to take in order to earn a return. That return grows the amount of money available to bless others. When we approach money with the firm belief that God owns it all, God can trust us with His resources knowing that we will use them to advance His Kingdom.

There is a second important lesson in this parable. Even though the servants started with different amounts, the master responded to each one, "Well done, good and faithful servant! You have been faithful with a few things; I will put you in charge of many things. Come and share your master's happiness!" (Matthew 25:21, 23).

It doesn't matter how much money we start with. It doesn't matter where on the financial wealth axis you find yourself today. Our faithfulness to save and invest in a way that honors God is much more important than the amount of money we have. Starting with more money makes accumulation easier, but it also makes the temptation to hoard greater. Keeping the faithful attitude that it's all God's money and being open to His direction on how to use it is the key.

Saving can also keep you from going into (more) debt. When we went through the Crown Financial Ministries bible study as a couple, we had another engaged couple from our church join us who were getting married right after the study was set to end. When we got to the week on debt, that couple asked the group, "Does this mean we shouldn't put our honeymoon on a credit card?" They already knew the answer to that question, but as a group we helped them come up with different options for their honeymoon. First, they chose a wonderful alternative honeymoon location that they liked as much as their original plan but cost half the price. Second, they chose to save up for the trip. They took extra odd jobs on weekends and worked together. As they saw their savings get closer and closer to their goal, their relationship strengthened. Instead of starting their marriage with more debt, they began their marriage having worked faithfully together to save for their honeymoon.

Debt can add so much stress, especially in the context of a marriage. Saving, when both spouses are working together as a team, can build a stronger relationship.

Ultimately, saving and surrendering everything you have to God is a powerful act of trust in the name of obedience. Obedience is the currency of faith. It's faith in action. It's following through in loving trust, saying, *Okay,*

Lord. I may not fully understand, but I know You are good. So I trust You anyway.

Whatever the Lord is calling you to do, we invite you to do it today. There are overarching biblical principles for finance and stewardship, but God may have a specific word for you today. What is God calling you to do with all you have as you surrender it to Him? God is faithful and true. As you step out in obedience and trust, watch what the Lord will do in and through you.

Spiritual Fruit Inventory: Saving vs. Hoarding

Love: Do you love God so much that you would sell all your possessions and give the money away if He asked you to? What would be the hardest thing for you to give up?

Joy: Think about the time in your life that you were filled with the most joy. What role did money play in that joy?

Peace: Do you experience God's peace regardless of how much money is in your bank account? What do you need to surrender to God in order to get to that place of peace? Write it down, and if you're ready, surrender it over to God. If you're not there yet, pray for God's peace to fill your heart and help you to surrender control.

Patience: One of the best ways to save is by being consistent over a long period of time. Get-rich-quick schemes rarely work. How patiently and consistently are you saving?

Kindness: Are you being kind to your family and the others around you as you save? Saving takes discipline and boundaries. But when the Holy Spirit is leading you, you can still be kind, even when it means saying "No" to those you love.

Goodness: Saving is a good thing. It allows you the freedom and flexibility to bless others and be even more generous in the long run. Is your saving producing good for those around you or causing harm?

Faithfulness: Are you being faithful in setting money aside? It's easy to fall into the temptation to spend when you're working to save. At the same time, are you being faithful to God when He puts a pressing need on your heart and calls you to deviate from your plan? Remember, faithfulness to God comes first, so as you faithfully save, continue to surrender all that you have to the Lord.

Gentleness: Are you being gentle with yourself and others? You may not do it perfectly all the time, but keep moving in the right direction. On the flip side, when saving becomes an obsession, it tends to turn toward hoarding.

Self-control: Saving is an act of self-control. It's saying "No" to short-term wants in order to accomplish a long-term goal. Where are you struggling with self-control financially? What boundaries or accountability can you put in place to help you where you're weakest?

God, here is where I am on this journey. If I am really honest, here are the areas of my life, my time, my resources where I have held back and been unwilling to surrender to You: ____________________. As scary as it is, and regardless of what you ask me to do, I surrender these areas to You. It all belongs to You, Lord. I trust You. Please help me where I'm afraid and when I doubt. I want to grow in my own faith by trusting you more so that I can help others.

In Jesus's name, Amen.

CHAPTER THREE

The world's money says, "Squander Me." God's money says, "Spend Me."

"It is not your salary that makes your rich; it's your spending habits"

Charles A. Jaffe

"Squander" is not a word we see used in marketing. *Come waste your money here. Great money-pit opportunity! Give us your money and we will give you something that will break, become obsolete, or require even more money to maintain!*

That kind of language would not sell a product, but, as with most things we buy, that is usually what will happen. So why do we squander money? As Isaiah 55:2 (ESV) asks, "Why do you spend your money for that which is not bread, and your labor for that which does not satisfy?"

God has a different invitation for us when it comes to how we use money: Spend it wisely. Money itself is not evil. Besides earning, saving, and giving, money is also used for spending—it's a tool. The key here is not overindulging or squandering, but to use it with discretion, a habit that goes against our consumer-driven culture. John Wesley called early Methodists to spend only on the "basics."

Though times have changed, the definition of "basics" still may be different for everyone. The basics could be health, education, and investments for the future. Wesley hoped that if early Methodists could spend money on their essential needs, they would have money left over to give. Could it be that financial hardships for Christ-followers and even churches are signs that they are living beyond their means? What would it look like if money was used as a tool rather than squandered? What if Christians lived within their means and avoided debt?

Wesley did not become a spiritual giant and benevolent man of God overnight. His outlook on finances was shaped by what Roz calls "memorizing the pain." When a young child touches a hot stove, of course they will get burned, but something else takes place—a painful memory is created in that short instance. Memorizing the pain means humans will do anything possible to avoid the painful situation again. For Wesley, it was the pain of seeing what his family endured when he was growing up that he wanted to avoid.

Samuel and Suzanna Wesley, John's parents, had 19 children, and experienced the pain of losing nine of them at childbirth. Samuel Wesley did not earn a high income as a clergyman and had trouble keeping the household afloat for his ten living children. As a result, the family was in a constant state of financial turmoil, leading to Samuel's arrest...twice because of his outstanding debts. The family situation was the picture Wesley had of finances. It was enough to motivate him to pursue educational endeavors, which ultimately landed him teaching opportunities with Oxford University and Lincoln College. Wesley quickly accumulated money in his pocket but did not want to model the poverty of his family. But without basic budgeting skills, he soon began to squander his money on card games, tobacco, and brandy. It was these spending habits that set the stage for a chance encounter that would change Wesley forever.[26]

Author Charles Wesley White describes an unforgettable lesson Wesley experienced one day in Oxford as recorded in his book, *What Wesley Preached and Practiced About Money*:

> *[Wesley] had just finished paying for some pictures for his room when one of the chambermaids came to his door. It was a cold winter day, and he noticed that she had nothing to protect her except a thin linen gown. He reached into his pocket to give her some money to buy a coat but found he had too little left. Immediately the thought struck him that the Lord was not pleased with the way he had spent his money. He asked himself, Will thy Master say, "Well done, good and faithful steward"? Thou hast adorned thy walls with the money which might have screened this poor creature from the cold! O justice! O mercy! Are not these pictures the blood of this poor maid?*[27]

Wesley never again wanted to experience the feeling of letting God or his brothers and sisters in Christ down. After

---

[26] Stephen Tomkins, *John Wesley: a Biography* (Lion Pub., 2003).

[27] Charles Edward White, *What Wesley Practiced and Preached About Money,* CT Pastors (Leadership Journal, January 1, 1987), https://www.christianitytoday.com/pastors/1987/winter/87l1027.html.

this painful moment, Wesley began to develop a theology and practice around money that would change his life and early Methodism. To begin, Wesley decided he would determine the bare minimum wages he needed to live on for one year. With an income of 30 pounds a year, Wesley determined he could live on 28 pounds and give away 2 pounds. Wesley's steady pace showed him that he could take another leap of faith as his second year of living frugally began. Wesley's income rose that second year, doubling from the previous year to 60 pounds. Though his income rose, Wesley kept his expenses the same at about 28 pounds, giving away 32 pounds that year. Year after year of Wesley's income growth, he continued to live on the minimum he set for himself while continuing to give away the rest.[28] Wesley's progress is carefully charted in a book called *The Accountability Connection* by Matt Friedman:

Year	Income	Living Expenses	To the Poor
First Year:	30 pounds	28 pounds (93%)	2 pounds (7%)
Second Year:	60 pounds	28 pounds (47%)	32 pounds (53%)
Third Year:	90 pounds	28 pounds (31%)	62 pounds (69%)
Fourth Year:	120 pounds	28 pounds (23%)	92 pounds (77%)
Eventually:	1,400 pounds+	30 pounds (2%)	1,400 pounds+ (98%)[29]

[28] Zack Van Zant, "The Radical Budget of John Wesley," Zack Van Zant, December 13, 2016, https://www.zackvanzant.com/blog/john-wesley-budget.

[29] Matt Friedeman, *The Accountability Connection* (Wheaton, IL: Victor Books, 1992), p. 12.

Wesley laid out four scriptural priorities when it comes to how early Methodists were to spend their hard-earned money:

I. **"Provide things needful for yourself and your family."** The basis for this priority is found in 1 Timothy 5:8, "Anyone who does not provide for their relatives, and especially for their own household, has denied the faith and is worse than an unbeliever." Wesley believed that it was necessary to provide "'a sufficiency of plain, wholesome food to eat, and clean raiment to put on,' as well as a place to live. The believer must also ensure that the family has enough to live on if something were to happen to the bread-winner."[30] Wesley said to provide what is needful for one's family. There is a difference between needs and wants. Wants and desires are not bad things in and of themselves, however, they must be held in tension, so money is not wasted unreasonably. It is no secret that today Americans have a spending problem and trouble distinguishing between needs and wants. It has become all too easy to put expenses on a credit card and figure out how to pay for purchases later, or open a department store card and pay it off over time with interest. Americans have close to a whopping $900 billion in credit card debt, carried by approximately 41 percent of American households.[31] The issue of credit card debt doesn't discriminate, either. Even those in higher income brackets have credit card debt.

---

30 "Four Lessons on Money: Christian History Magazine," Christian History Institute, n.d., https://christianhistoryinstitute.org/magazine/article/four-lessons-on-money.

31 Marcie Geffner, "15 Shocking Credit Card Debt Statistics," CardRates.com, August 10, 2020, https://www.cardrates.com/advice/shocking-credit-card-debt-statistics/.

II. **"Having food and raiment, let us therewith be content."** This priority comes directly from 1 Timothy 6:8. Wesley shares, "It plainly follows, whatever is more than these is, in the sense of the Apostle, riches; whatever is above the plain necessities, or at most convenience of life. Whoever has sufficient food to eat, and raiment to put on, with a place to lay his head, and something over, is rich."[32] Wesley hits on the importance of contentment in small things that can be quickly taken for granted, like food and clothing. One notices that Wesley does not specify what kind of food and clothing he's talking about here. Our culture has a way of elevating food and clothing styles that are extravagant—what we picture a successful person eating or wearing. Contentment in small things, or even in the bigger details of life, does not come naturally to human beings. Contentment is a learned behavior that doesn't happen overnight or just because someone decides to follow Jesus. The apostle Paul echoes this exact sentiment while he was imprisoned in Rome in Philippians 4:11, "I am not saying this because I am in need, for I have learned to be content whatever the circumstances." Learning contentment is a life-long lesson that few master, but once learned, it can yield unbelievable fruit.

III. **"Provide things honest in the sight of all men"** and "Owe no man anything." This priority is based on two verses: Romans 12:17 commands, "Do not repay anyone evil for evil. Be careful to do what is right in the eyes of everyone." And Romans 13:8 instructs, "Let no

---

32 John Wesley, "On the Danger of Increasing Riches," West Blocton Bible Methodist Church, accessed September 5, 2020, http://www.wbbm.org/john-wesley-sermons/serm-126.htm.

debt remain outstanding, except the continuing debt to love one another, for whoever loves others has fulfilled the law."[33] We should avoid debt and live above reproach in all we do. This starts with spending responsibly and conducting business ethically.

IV. **"Do good to them that are of the household of faith"** and **"As you have opportunity, do good unto all men."** Based on Galatians 6:10, Wesley instructs believers to care for their fellow Christian brothers and sisters as they are able to care for all people. We are to spend what God has placed in our hands to bless others. Wesley goes on to say, "The Lord will then inquire: Was thou accordingly a general benefactor to mankind? feeding the hungry, clothing the naked, comforting the sick, assisting the stranger, relieving the afflicted, according to their various necessities? Was thou eyes to the blind, and feet to the lame? a father to the fatherless, and a husband to the widow?"[34] Basically, were you being the hands and feet of Jesus, reflecting Christ's love with how you live and how you use your resources?

Not every financial situation is clear. There are times where God's Word does not provide specific instructions on what to do with your finances. Wesley offered several questions to help Christians discern how to spend wisely and avoid squandering their money:

---

[33] John Wesley, "Sermon 'The Danger of Riches," ed. Thomas Jackson, WordsOf-Wesley, accessed September 5, 2020, http://www.wordsofwesley.com/libtext.cfm?srm=87.

[34] John Wesley, The Wesley Center Online: Sermon 51 - The Good Steward, Wesley Center Online, accessed September 5, 2020, http://wesley.nnu.edu/john-wesley/the-sermons-of-john-wesley-1872-edition/sermon-51-the-good-steward/.

- In spending this money, am I acting as if I owned it, or am I acting as the Lord's trustee?
- What Scripture requires me to spend this money in this way?
- Can I offer up this purchase as a sacrifice to the Lord?
- Will God reward me for this expenditure at the resurrection of the just?

Finally, for the believer who is perplexed, Wesley suggests this prayer before making a purchase:

> *Lord, Thou seest I am going to expend this sum on that food, apparel, or furniture. And Thou knowest I act therein with a single eye, as a steward of thy goods, expending this portion of them thus, in persuance of the design thou hadst in entrusting me with them. Thou knowest I do this in obedience to Thy Word, as Thou commandest, and because Thou commandest it. Let this, I beseech Thee, be an holy sacrifice, acceptable through Jesus Christ! And give me a witness in myself, that for this labor of love I shall have a recompense when Thou rewardest every man according to his works.*[35]

If all we have belongs to God, then how we spend money should glorify God, also. It is not just about tithing 10 percent back to God. If we are stewarding that money wisely, the way the other 90 percent is spent matters just as much as our tithe. If the Lord is guiding you in your

---

[35] John Wesley, The Wesley Center Online: Sermon 50 - The Use Of Money, The Wesley Center Online, accessed September 5, 2020, http://wesley.nnu.edu/john-wesley/the-sermons-of-john-wesley-1872-edition/sermon-50-the-use-of-money/.

spending, some aspects of your spending will look similar to others who are also being guided by the Lord, but many things will be unique to the relationship you have with God.

Some similar principles that all Christian spending should reflect:

God is God. Possessions should not be idols.

As Wesley asked, "Can I offer up this purchase as a sacrifice to the Lord?" If your focus is to accumulate more, bigger, or better, that focus tends to be a worldly one. God cares more about your heart than anything. If your purchases create an idol of stuff in your life, that puts created things over and above the Creator. If possessions start to possess you, then you are no longer the owner. Your stuff now owns you.

Beware of idols.

If you notice your heart lusting after something (a new car, piece of technology, article of clothing, etc.), confess those motives. Ask God to help you worship the Lord over that item. If you already own it, ask the Lord if it is safe spiritually for you to keep it. If you do not own it yet, turn your attention to God instead of that item, and ask God if there is something He would have you use that money for instead. Your heart is what matters most.

Some possessions can be held by some Christians without being an idol, while they would cause another to stumble. There might be a Christian safely owning a second home and using it to bring family together or blessing others with a vacation getaway who could not otherwise afford one. Another Christian might make that same home into an idol, or it could stretch that person financially in unhealthy ways, causing them to take on extreme amounts of debt. Each Christian is unique, but any possession that becomes an idol is a stumbling block in your faith.

Spending should be within your budget.

If you are spending more money than you make, it is time to cut back. If you are spending to the point where you are not able to give, are not able to save, and going into increasing levels of debt, there is a problem. Now, some may need to also increase income, but there are often spending cuts that can be made to limit spending to necessities.

Where are your weaknesses? Where do you tend to splurge? Find ways to set a budget for that area of your spending and set up accountability measures to keep you within your budget. In extreme circumstances, you might need to cut up all of your credit cards and go with cash only. Others may be able to only use cash for certain areas of their budget, like eating out, shopping, etc. If online shopping is a weakness, you might need to fast from looking at certain sites. The more you shop, the more likely you are to spend. Do not tempt yourself. Consider a spending fast.

You might also need to declutter. Sometimes simply clearing out a space reminds you of the things you already have. Either use those items or remove them from your home.

Watch for expenses on maintaining possessions you do not use.

The storage industry continues to grow. We buy and buy and do not have enough space to store everything we have. If you have things in storage you have not used for more than a year, talk honestly with a trusted friend about what it would look like for you to sell or donate what is inside. More cars mean more expenses. More homes mean more repairs, more insurance, and more utilities. Bigger homes take more money to maintain as well. If you had less, would you spend less simply by having less to maintain?

Your budget should reflect your values.

You can tell a lot about what a person values by the way they spend their time and money. Take a look at where your money went last month. If someone looked at your bank statement or credit card bill, would they see your love for the Lord? What would they see? If anything does not line up with what you say you value, consider cutting it out.

Use subscriptions or remove subscriptions.

It's easy to sign up for something for a low monthly rate of $x, but those purchases add up quickly. Are you using those subscriptions? Those gym memberships, online movie streaming services, music services, news services, whatever they may be? If you are not using them, cut them out. Or do you have multiple services that are similar? What would it look like to cut out one subscription and reinvest that money into something that is a spending priority for you?

Use your spending to value the laborer.

This one takes a little more work and, at times, a little more expense, but fair and ethical trade organizations are growing. There is a movement to provide products that pay the laborer a living wage, that care for the environment, and use your consumer dollars in a way you can feel better about. It's easy to focus on ourselves and what we want, but the Bible calls us to love our neighbor as ourselves. How can you value the laborer who made the products you buy? What spending changes could you make to support local, pay laborers a living wage, and/or reduce the impact of your consumption on the environment?

Live beneath your means.

You might be thinking, *I cannot afford the things I need as it is. How do I live beneath my means*? As you review your expenses, build in margin by cutting back in any area that does not line up with your faith and is not necessary. The more you do this over the long-term, the better you are able to live on less, freeing up more money for giving and saving.

* * *

The challenge is lifestyle creep—the more you make, the more you tend to spend. You have the money, so you buy a bigger home, a nicer car, fancier clothing, etc. These things in and of themselves are not bad, but watch for the overall trend. Continue to surrender everything to the Lord, and watch for what God might be calling you to do.

Dr. Renee Lockey did just this, and she was surprised by what God told her. An OB/GYN at the age of 37, Renee had accomplished all she had planned, but she also felt like something was missing. She thought that the more money she had, the more freedom she would feel, but she was not content. One day, while out on a run with God, she heard God tell her, *I want you to work like a doctor and I want you to live like a nurse.* That led her to live on a quarter of her salary. It took her time to learn to live on a budget again. Renee also reprioritized her giving and stopped worrying about saving as aggressively. She realized her peace was not in the amount of money she saved, but in the freedom that came from obeying the Lord and trusting God with all she had. In living beneath her means, the emptiness disappeared and Renee felt God filling her up to overflowing with His peace and joy.[36]

Spending is part of living for most everyone. Spending money is not evil in and of itself. Look to God in your spending. How can you honor the Lord with everything you have, including the money you spend?

Be free. Money cannot buy you freedom. Money is always a means of owning—owning people, owning animals, or owning property. Debt can put you in prison; if not literally

---

[36] "Renee Lockey," Generous Giving, accessed November 22, 2020, https://generousgiving.org/media/videos/renee-lockey.

then figuratively. Money alone cannot buy you the freedom you want. You will always be a slave either to money, someone else you owe money to, or to the Lord. In God, you find true freedom and true happiness. When you look to the Lord, you learn that *Heaven–not Earth–is your home,* so you do not worry about earthly treasures and accumulating boatloads of things. As John 8:36 explains, "if the Son sets you free, you will be free indeed." God has to be the one to fill that void in your heart and life. No money or possession can ever do that. Freedom comes from Christ alone.

We invite you to complete the following sentences:

Being in debt makes me feel ...

When I imagine being debt free, I feel ...

If I were debt free, I would use the money I was paying on debt to ...

Create a sheet to list all of your outstanding debts. Next to each, list the remaining amount that you owe, the interest rate, monthly payment date, and minimum monthly payment. Leave a spot to note which you are going to attack first. At the bottom, add up the amount remaining column to calculate the total of your debt outstanding. Also add up the minimum monthly payments column. Here's an example you can use:

Debt Repayment Worksheet

Instructions: 1) List all debts owed (credit cards, auto loans, student loans, mortgages, Lines of Credit, bank loans, loans from family or friends, past due medical bills, other past due bills, retirement loans (from IRA, 401k, etc.), business loans, and any other debt or loans outstanding.

2) Organize so all credit cards are first, then all other debts with an interest rate greater than 10%, then all debts other than your mortgage. Your mortgage, if you have one, goes last.

3) Within each of those groupings, list the debt with the lowest balance (total amount owed/remaining) first, increasing to the highest balance.

4) Continue to make monthly payments on all of the debts and put any extra money toward the first debt on your list until that one is completely gone. Then put the amount you were paying on that one plus the minimum payment on debt #2 toward the 2nd debt. As you go, the amount you pay on each individual debt will increase ("snowball") and gain momentum.

5) If you don't have enough to cover payments or any extra to knock out debts, you'll have to work on your budget and consider selling items or increasing income to come up with the money to repay.

Debt #	Name of Debt (ex. Chase Visa Card)	Total amount owed (total remaining)	Interest Rate	Minimum Monthly Payment	Monthly Due Date
1)					
2)					
3)					
4)					
5)					
6)					
7)					
8)					
9)					
10)					
11)					
12)					
13)					
14)					
15)					
16)					
17)					
18)					

Total Due: $ **Monthly Due: $**

As much as you're able, you should set aside some of your budget for paying off debt. Here are some additional ways to pay off debt faster:

- Sell the item you owe money on, especially if you do not need it or could replace it with a less expensive item (i.e., a car, house, boat, motorcycle).
- Apply any financial gifts, bonuses, tax refunds, or other additional income to debt repayment.
- Take an extra side job and apply all that income toward debt repayment.

Tools along the way:

- Budget – If you do not set a spending plan to help you live within your means, you will most likely go further into debt, and you will not be able to get your existing spending under control in order to pay off the debt you do have.
- Rewards – It helps to celebrate and have rewards to look forward to along the way. Pick a reward that you will use to celebrate paying off each debt and reaching different milestones along the way. That incentive can help motivate you in your journey to become debt free.

God has set you free by paying all of your outstanding debts of sin on the cross with the blood of Jesus Christ. You are free. Do not stumble in darkness when you have the light of life inside you. Ask God to shine a light into your heart to search you, even in the area of your possessions, to see if there is any wicked way in you and lead you in the way everlasting (Psalm 139:23-34). Let the Lord show you where you are sinning and gently lead you to repentance. God's goal is not to shame you, but to draw you close to His love. The Lord wants you to walk in perfect love and freedom, and that starts with coming to God—offering up all that you are and all that you have. God will not take it from you, God will show you what you need to surrender to Him.

What has become an idol for you? What would you have a hard time giving away? Come and surrender. Watch how God transforms that item. Watch for freedom to enter in.

Does your house have a hold on you? What would it look like to invite others in? To let them live there, find refuge there?

You might not have to sell something or give it away to be free, but as you listen, God will speak to your heart. God knows you by name. He knit you together in your mother's womb. He knows what's a temptation and what has a hold on your heart. God will guide you in letting go. Be free as God made you to be.

Greed? Jealousy? What makes you keep spending wastefully? What hole are you trying to fill? If you sit still for a minute, what bubbles up? How long could you go without buying anything new (excluding groceries)? Can you fast from buying for a period of 40 days? A year? How long could you go?

What is your initial reaction to this challenge? What do you feel like you would be missing? What could you do with that money instead if you were not spending as much?

Maybe you could be more generous, pay down debt, or save for the future. There are so many good things you could do if you stopped spending on needless things.

No matter how we grew up or what setting we currently find ourselves in financially, we're forced to wrestle with a culture focused on money and possessions. To be free means we have to reject the common myths our consumer-driven culture feeds us.

Myth 1: Having more things will make me happier.

The fact is, things *can* bring happiness. But the problem is that happiness is temporary. Things do make you happy. If you get a gift you love, you are happy about it. However, it does not last, and after a while the thrill goes away, the excitement fades, and boredom sets in because things never change but we always will. We get bored with things that do not change, so we want to buy new, redecorate, or have the latest model with the newest features. What did you get for Christmas last year? Are you still thrilled over last year's gift? Chances are this year you want the bigger, better, nicer model, or something else brand new.

Myth 2: Having more things will make me more important.

There is this idea promoted by commercials, shows, magazines, and ads that says if I have money and nice things, then I must be important. The misconception here is this: I am what I own, my valuables determine my value, and if I have little then I must be worth little. Since I want to be liked and respected, I must continually keep getting more and more and more. I have to keep up with the Joneses. Don't worry about keeping up with the Joneses—they just refinanced and took on more debt.

Since we've been married, we've owned three houses together. The first Callie owned before we got married. It was a three-bedroom, two-bath house in one of the nicest areas of Lexington, KY. That first house was only about five minutes from her parents' home because she was told by her realtor that she should buy in that neighborhood. It's the three rules of real estate: Location, Location, Location. Callie thought having a nice house was important, but the house was honestly more than she could afford on her own, and she had to keep dipping further and further into her savings just to cover the mortgage payments each month. When we got married, we knew we would be able to afford the payments better with two incomes. Still, Roz kept challenging Callie about not needing that nice of a house. For Callie, that house was a really hard thing to give up.

Myth 3: Having more things will make me more secure.

"If I could just achieve financial independence ..." Have you heard that one? As if financial independence is the goal of life. The truth is, the more you have, the more *insecure* you'll be because you now have more to worry about. The more you have, the more time and energy it takes to maintain it. The more you have, the more insurance you have to pay to insure it.

Living the American dream means we are asleep to the reality of what is taking place in our world.

Real security can only be found when you place your security in something that cannot be taken away from you. If you put your security in things, things can be ripped away from you a million different ways—legally or illegally. You must have security in something that cannot be taken away from you, and the only thing that cannot be taken away from you is your relationship with God. Even our families can and will be taken away from us, but God never will.

If you are trusting in your pension plan for security, that pension plan becomes your god. But if you are trusting in God, He is your God.

Financial worries are something Christians have been wrestling with for centuries. We can see this play out through Jesus's words in Matthew 6:25-34:

> *"That is why I tell you not to worry about everyday life—whether you have enough food and drink, or enough clothes to wear. Isn't life more than food, and your body more than clothing? Look at the birds. They don't plant or harvest or store food in barns, for your heavenly Father feeds them. And aren't you far more valuable to him than they are? Can all your worries add a single moment to your life?*
>
> *"And why worry about your clothing? Look at the lilies of the field and how they grow.*
>
> *They don't work or make their clothing, yet Solomon in all his glory was not dressed as beautifully as they are. And if God cares so wonderfully for wildflowers that are here*

> *today and thrown into the fire tomorrow, he will certainly care for you. Why do you have so little faith?*
>
> *"So don't worry about these things, saying, 'What will we eat? What will we drink? What will we wear?' These things dominate the thoughts of unbelievers, but your heavenly Father already knows all your needs. Seek the Kingdom of God above all else, and live righteously, and he will give you everything you need.*
>
> *"So don't worry about tomorrow, for tomorrow will bring its own worries. Today's trouble is enough for today."*

Today some of us are feeling those very real worries of having enough food to eat, clothes to wear, and shelter to live in. Others are struggling with the pressures our culture adds to having the right clothes, eating the fancy health foods, or keeping up with those around us. We have made choices to try to keep up with how our culture says we should live, and financially, we can't do it anymore. The debt adds up, and the stuff does not make us feel any happier, any more important, or any more secure. Yet, we still want more.

We have looked at the myths our consumer-driven culture feeds us, now it's time to explore some ways we as Christ-followers can follow Christ in the midst of this consumer-driven culture. Callie and I struggle with this way of living a lot, but here are some things we have found that help us live simply and live free.

Resist Comparing What You Have to Others

Just when you're starting to feel good with what you have, you look over your shoulder and somebody just got the newer model.

We love to compare ourselves to our peers, saying, "I don't have as much as so-and-so." But have you ever been on a mission trip in a third-world country? So often we as Christians in first-world countries go to a third-world country thinking we're going to do good and help so many people. But in reality, the trip ends up helping us more. Experiencing life in a third-world country gives us a wakeup call—seeing the joy and freedom these Christians have, even without excessive wealth. We come back disgusted with our accumulation of money and possessions, but eventually we return to normal life. We are back around our peers, seeing constant advertisements, and we forget our disgust for material possession, becoming desensitized once again. We all too quickly conform to the world around us.

That first house Callie owned and thought she needed to be happy was so hard to give up because it was possessing her. Callie worried what other people would think when we sold it to move to a more affordable home. The more Callie wrestled with owning the house, the more she realized that though the house may have fit her life before she married Roz, and may have fit with the people she had grown up around, owning that house was not congruent with the call God had placed on our lives. Our call has been to lead churches that bring people together across diverse backgrounds, and this house did more to divide than unite.

So, we sold the house and bought a three-bedroom, two-bath house for half the price in downtown Lexington, located in a neighborhood between the two campuses of our church. We quickly realized that we were happier without as much debt. And even though the location was not as desirable in the eyes of many, it was a better location for God's call on our lives.

A few years later, God called us to Ginghamsburg United Methodist Church in the Dayton, OH area. We were going to spend those first years focusing on The Point campus in Trotwood, OH. We knew that to do the ministry well, we would need to be fully invested in Trotwood, so we bought a three-bedroom, two-bath house in Trotwood for a third of the price of our old house in Lexington. With each move, we have realized that as much as location, location, location matters from a real estate perspective, being in the location God's calling you to matters so much more. Having the nicest, most expensive house just means bigger mortgage payments, and what actually matters is God's call on our lives. That call is different for each of us and may change in different seasons, but whatever that call is, we will find more joy being in the center of God's will. But that requires resisting the temptation to compare ourselves with others.

Rejoice in What I Do Have

Contentment is not a natural trait. It must be learned. We invite you to enroll in the school of contentment today. *God, help me learn to be content with what I have. Forgive me for jealously wanting more. Thank you for all you have already given me.*

Paul went to this school of contentment. In Philippians 4:11-12, he says, "I have learned to be content whatever the circumstances. I know what it is to be in need, and I know what it is to have plenty."

G. K. Chesterton echoes Paul, saying, "There are two ways to get enough. One is to continue to accumulate more and more. The other is to desire less."[37] Contentment is the key, but you can easily get off the track.

The verses from Matthew 6 call us not to worry about tomorrow, but to rejoice in the food and clothes we have for today, and the God who cares for us intimately. As verse 30 says, "And if God cares so wonderfully for wildflowers that are here today and thrown into the fire tomorrow, he will certainly care for you."

It's amazing how much better kids do this than adults. Callie was really close to her grandpa. She always called him "Honey" because that's what her grandma called him and, as a small child, Callie thought that was her grandpa's

---

[37] GK Chesterton. *GK Chesteron's The Crimes Of England: "There are two ways to get enough. One is to continue to accumulate more and more. The other is to desire less."* (A Word to The Wise, 2013).

name. It stuck. Honey was a storyteller. He loved to tell a story about Callie as a child. Her birthday was coming up, and Honey asked her if she would like a new dress.

Callie replied, "I already have a dress, Honey."

So he asked, "What about a new stuffed animal?"

Callie had a favorite stuffed bunny rabbit that was pretty worn out, but she replied, "I already have a bunny, Honey."

Callie was happy and content with what she did have, but somewhere along the way she grew up, as all children do. Materialism creeps in, and we forget to be grateful and rejoice in what we already have. Jesus never tells little children to grow up, but He does call us to have a childlike faith. We need to be more like children, rejoicing in what God has already provided rather than comparing ourselves to others.

Return The First Ten Percent Back to God

This practice is called tithing. Matthew 6:33 exhorts us to "Seek the Kingdom of God above all else, and live righteously, and he will give you everything you need." The King James version of this same verse says, "But seek ye first the kingdom of God, and his righteousness; and all these things shall be added unto you." The purpose of tithing is to teach you to always put God first.

God does not need our money, but He wants our heart, and where your treasure is there your heart will be also.

Tithing is a way to test our own hearts. Does our money possess us, or are we free to give it up? Giving is an antidote to greed. It breaks the chains of materialism. It forces us to step out in faith and trust God. It is defying that myth that more money will make you more secure, and saying, *God, I am secure in You. I trust you more than the number of dollars in my bank account.* But tithing can be scary. When each month can be a struggle to stretch a paycheck, making the leap of faith to seek God first and tithe sounds crazy. But remember the God we serve, the God who is a loving Father and already knows all your needs. We do not know what tomorrow holds, but God does, and He provides.

Satan would love to hold you back with fear, but do not let him. That is why rejoicing in what we do have and all the ways God has provided is so important. Rejoicing is what allows us to step out in faith and return 10 percent. We will talk more about giving in the next chapter, but when you plan your spending, it is important to first set aside a percentage of that income for the Lord.

Not only is giving Biblical, but it is also something that has helped us live financially free and follow Christ throughout our marriage, even when our consumer-driven culture tells us not to. Tithing has been hardest in the times when we've been stretched thin. We had to keep remembering that God is faithful, and choosing to seek first the Kingdom of God.

Refocus: Hold What You Do Have With an Open Hand

What, if in addition to giving generously back to God at least 10 percent, we gave Him access to the other 90 percent of our income and all our stuff? What if the stuff we already have was dedicated toward doing good and went toward becoming rich in good deeds? What if we were truly willing to share it all?

In each of those three-bedroom, two-bath houses we've owned, we have made space for a guest room. And in each of those three houses, we have been able to use the guest bedroom at various times to have friends who needed a place to stay live with us for free. Stuff gains value when it is open for God to use in ministry.

* * *

What is God saying to you today? What do you need to do to respond to Him? God is calling each of us to live financially free and to follow Him in a consumer-driven culture, but that call looks different for each of us.

Do you need to resist comparing yourself to others? Perhaps you need to stop a magazine subscription or curb the amount of time you spend browsing Facebook.

Maybe you know you need to start rejoicing and thanking God for everything He has blessed you with rather than focusing on what you do not have. Can you start each day this week by thanking God for three things He has given you?

Maybe you have never taken that leap of faith to return 10 percent to God, and today is the day to start tithing. Put your trust in God, and see how He provides.

Maybe you need to refocus and surrender the possessions to God that are possessing you. Make a list of the items you are offering up to Him as the owner to use however He can for ministry and the Kingdom.

Take a moment now to be silent and write down the one thing you feel called to do in response to God's call of freedom on your life.

* * *

Like we wrote about in the last chapter, one of Callie's prerequisites for marrying Roz was going through a Crown Financial Ministries study together. Doing a financial bible study is an important tool for any individual or couple, but it was so powerful for us to get on the same page about how we were going to manage the resources God placed in our hands.

Whenever Roz conducts any premarital counseling, there is always a section he includes on finances. To help reinforce the teachings Roz has learned in Scripture with practical applications, Roz invites Callie along to help facilitate the discussion. In a recent study conducted by Utah State University, the study said, "fighting about finances is a top predictor of divorce, with couples who fight frequently being 30 percent more likely to divorce than those who rarely argue."[38]

During the counseling we ask engaged couples questions like: "How was money used when you were growing up?" "How did your parents or the people who raised you engage in the topic and practice of money?" "What is your philosophy around finances, and what are your goals?" The big question that receives a lot of discussion is, "how much debt do you have?" According to a study conducted by Fidelity on couples and money, "More than half of all couples go into their partnerships with debt, and 40 percent say that this financial burden ends up having a negative impact on their relationships."[39]

When we pose that question about how much debt each person has going into the marriage, the answers are often troubling. Some couples have no idea how much debt they have and cannot even put a ballpark figure on it. Or worse, they have not talked to each other about what kind of debt they are bringing into their marriage—leading to some necessary discussion. The other question and challenge we pose to these couples revolves around budgeting:

---

[38] Jean Chatzky, "Why Getting out of Debt Can Save Your Marriage," NBCNews.com, December 15, 2018, https://www.nbcnews.com/better/business/want-marital-bliss-divorce-debt-not-each-other-ncna948131.

[39] "'Til Debt Do Us Part: Nearly Half of Couples Concerned about Debt Also Name Money as Their Biggest Relationships Challenge," Fidelity Investments, June 26, 2018, https://newsroom.fidelity.com/press-releases/news-details/2018/Til-debt-do-us-part-Nearly-half-of-couples-concerned-about-debt-also-name-money-as-their-biggest-relationships-challenge/default.aspx.

how to develop a budget and do some financial planning with hard numbers to know what their projected joint income and expenses will be going into the marriage. In addition to the ambiguity around debt, some couples told us that they planned to continue to operate with different bank accounts since it's easier and that's what they were used to as singles. We encourage couples to build a good foundation on Christ and plan accordingly. When two people become one flesh, their income is one, their expenses are one, and their debt is one, so they need to act and operate financially as one, too.

Rule of Life for Your Finances

A "Rule of Life" is a concept that came out of the fourth century monastic movement. Rule of Life practices have continued since then, and many Christians outside the monastery practice one as a way of setting intentions. Pastor and author Peter Scazzero has some great material on creating a Rule of Life in his book, *Emotionally Healthy Spirituality: It's Impossible to Be Spiritually Mature, While Remaining Emotionally Immature.* Scazzero defines a Rule of Life as "an intentional, conscious plan to keep God at the center of everything we do... The starting point and foundation of any Rule is a desire to be with God and to love him."[40] Despite being called a rule, a Rule of Life is

---

[40] Peter Scazzero. *Emotionally Healthy Spirituality: It's Impossible to Be Spiritually Mature, While Remaining Emotionally Immature,* (Zondervan: 2017), p. 196.

not meant to be restrictive, rather it's a way to keep the main thing the main thing in the midst of competing distractions in the world around us. Scazzero has four primary sections in his Rule of Life-Prayer, Relationships, Work, and Rest-and encourages Christians to set practices that will prioritize each of those important areas (ex: daily quiet time with the Lord, family meals, calling parents, writing, practicing a weekly Sabbath). The options can be as diverse as the people God created.

What would it look like for you to develop a Financial Rule of Life with the sections Earn, Save, Spend, and Give? What practices would you choose to define those areas? While your Financial Rule of Life will be unique to you and may change in different seasons of life, here is our Picardo Family Rule of Life for this season as an example to help get you started:

Earn:

- We both work full-time for United Theological Seminary
- Roz is co-pastor of Mosaic Church and Callie is on the preaching team
- We both speak, coach, consult, and write
- Earn a fair wage
- Willing to sacrifice income in seasons to advance the Kingdom
- Do not work to the detriment of health, family, or key relationships

Save:

- Save for retirement so that one day we can do ministry without the need for income
- Keep an emergency fund with at least three months of income
- Save for big purchases
- Diversify our investments and save responsibly for the long-term, avoiding get-rich-quick schemes

Spend:

- Never spend more than we earn
- Live modestly within our means so that we can give generously and save intentionally
- Avoid debt, with the exception of an affordable home mortgage
- Prioritize education
- Experiences over accumulating stuff
- Health is important – spend on healthy food and exercise
- At least one family vacation annually

Give:

- Giving is a priority for our family
- Give at least 10 percent to our church
- Give above and beyond to Christian organizations advancing the Kingdom

These sections of our Financial Rule of Life are a way of prioritizing our intentions. If a new opportunity comes our way, we look at it in light of the values we have already set. Another opportunity may come up for earning money, but if it means we would be working to the detriment of health or family, we evaluate whether it's time to give up one of the other things we are doing to earn income, either permanently or for a season. For instance, when Roz started working full-time at United Theological Seminary while continuing to co-pastor Mosaic, he cut back his ongoing coaching relationships. We have both said no to other opportunities because it would have taken us away from our family too many times in rapid succession.

Another giving opportunity may come up, and we evaluate our existing giving commitments to see if any should change. An opportunity to go on a trip may also come up. For instance, Callie was able to go to the Holy Land for free on a trip with United donors. We wanted to experience that trip of a lifetime together, so we started saving for Roz to be able to go with her, cutting back in other areas to set funds aside for that experience.

There are also creative ways to accomplish your goals. For birthdays and Christmas, we have asked our family to spend less on toys for the kids in favor of investing in a college education fund for each one. While we cannot aggressively save for their college education because of other financial priorities, the willingness of grandparents to help in that area frees us up to care for other needs. Our own education has been a priority as well, and we have been able to take advantage of scholarships and continuing education programs from our employers to assist with education costs.

Not everyone will have the same opportunities as others, but don't be afraid to think outside the box. Not every financial priority has to be accomplished with the swipe of a credit card or the writing of a check.

When we first moved to Dayton, Callie gave up the job she loved for Roz to accept a new employment opportunity. As we listened to God's call, the Lord made it clear that Callie was not supposed to rush into full-time employment. During that year, Callie volunteered and built relationships in our new community. She also joined a TimeBank co-op. Members could post needs or offer skills and pay for it with time. Callie offered healthy cooking lessons and tutoring. She received garden help and a family photography session, among other things. No dollars were exchanged, only time.

Do you have a friend or neighbor you could set up a similar arrangement with? Maybe someone will watch your kids and you offer to mow their lawn and shovel their snow. Don't be afraid to get creative.

Around the first of the year, or any time our income changes substantially, we pray through and discuss our Rule of Life and budget for the year, asking God one primary question: *Lord, is there anything you would have us change so we can better honor You?*

Remember, a Rule of Life is meant to be a gift, not an onerous source of stress. Surrender all you have to the Lord, and watch how He will use it.

Spiritual Fruit Inventory: Spending vs. Squandering

Love: Look at your last credit card and bank statement. If someone examined those statements closely and knew nothing else about you, what would they identify as the things you love the most?

Joy: Do you find your joy in the Lord or do you look to shopping and new things to make you happy? If you turn to shopping, what are some new habits you can form to replace that need to self-medicate with shopping when you feel bored, lonely, sad, or anxious? How will you implement those new habits?

Peace: Consider adding this new practice before you spend money, especially bigger purchases (set a dollar threshold): Before spending, ask God whether you are supposed to buy that item now, wait, or go without it altogether. Pay attention to where you feel God's peace and where you feel unease about purchases.

Patience: Are you patient to wait on the Lord to provide, or do you feel the need to buy things immediately? Consider a 24-hour rule on bigger purchases—when you see something you want, wait until the next day to actually buy it. Try to avoid impulse purchases.

Kindness: Not all products are created equally. As you are able, choose products that pay the laborer a fair wage or reduce negative impacts on the environment. Be kind in your spending. What is one spending practice you could change to advocate for kindness with your purchasing power?

Goodness: What are some good things you want to spend your money on? What kinds of purchases line up with your faith and the things and people you value most? What is one intentional good gift you could purchase for someone this month that would bless that person?

Faithfulness: Are you faithful to God, yourself, and your family with the way you choose to use money? Are you spending it in ways that advance the Kingdom and provide for your needs and those of your family, or are you wasting it on selfish wants and things that do not matter? What is one area that you need to make a change in?

Gentleness: A Rule of Life is meant to guide you. Don't make it unbearably strict, but do make it intentional. Do you have a financial Rule of Life that gently guides you in the way you want to go? If not, take some time to write down a Rule of Life for your finances, include practices and priorities for your earning, saving, spending, and giving.

Self-control: Is your spending out of control? What is the area of your spending in which you are most likely to squander money? Pick one strategy to help you practice self-control in your spending.

God, I want to honor you in all that I am and all that I do, including the way I spend the money you have given me to steward. Help me to make wise decisions. I confess I have bought many things I should not have purchased. Please forgive me. Help me when I am weak to practice self-control. I do not want to squander money, but I do want to intentionally spend it to advance Your Kingdom and share Your love with the world around me.

CHAPTER FOUR

The world's money says, "Worship Me." God's money says, "Give Me."

As base a thing as money often is, yet it can be transmuted into everlasting treasure. It can be converted into food for the hungry and clothing for the poor. It can keep a missionary actively winning lost men to the light of the gospel and thus transmute itself into heavenly values. Any temporal possession can be turned into everlasting wealth. Whatever is given to Christ is immediately touched with immortality.

A.W. Tozer

At the beginning of Methodism, the early pioneers of this movement were in poverty. Then, something changed. John Wesley pointed out that in the 20, 30, or 40 years since they joined the society, many Methodists had become 20, 30, or even 100 times wealthier than they were when they first became Methodists. But with this increase in wealth came a decrease in godliness. They had fallen in love with their money and loved God even less than they did before. Some thought they had accumulated wealth on their own instead of viewing themselves as trustees of God's resources.[41]

---

[41] Dr. White, "Four Lessons on Money: Christian History Magazine," *Christian History Institute,* (1988), https://christianhistoryinstitute.org/magazine/article/four-lessons-on-money.

American Christians can learn a lot from this example. God is calling Christ-followers to steward their resources, and part of that stewardship is the act of generosity. There is a widely believed fallacy that on average, those who give the most in proportion to their income fall below the poverty line. However, in a recent study exploring who gives more in proportion to their income, economist Benjamin Priday concluded that "The most popularly cited measure of generosity is the proportion of a family's income that is donated. This is where the rich appear to be the stingiest. But this notion turns out to be incorrect: After limiting the distorting effect of the outliers, the share of income people give away is essentially flat across income levels."[42]

Generosity is the only antidote to potential greed and the worship of money, regardless of your income level. The act of generosity is not just for Christian individuals alone, but is also an activity that churches, networks, and denominations can participate in to extend their Kingdom-building work far beyond their circles.

Money the world's way wants to be worshiped. It is one of the most common idols in American culture today, but it was also a tempting idol in Jesus's time. Money is one of the most common things Jesus taught on. It's a prominent theme in His parables, and was an important topic in His

---

[42] Benjamin Priday, "Charitable Giving: Are the Rich Really Stingier than the Rest of Us?," Generosity Philly, accessed May 22, 2020, https://generocity.org/philly/2020/05/21/charitable-giving-are-the-rich-really-stingier-than-the-rest-of-us/.

Sermon on the Mount, where in Matthew 6:24, He teaches, "No one can serve two masters. Either you will hate the one and love the other, or you will be devoted to the one and despise the other. You cannot serve both God and money." That verse is sandwiched in between instructions on storing up riches in Heaven (giving) and trusting God for material provision on this Earth. The world says, worship money. It says store up treasure on this earth and trust money to provide for your earthly needs. If you are going to worship God, you have to stop trusting in your material wealth. Worship God by giving instead—storing up treasure in Heaven—so the loyalties of your heart will be there also. Who do you want to worship, God or money? You cannot serve both, so it's time to stop and make your decision right now.

In 1913, Dayton, OH experienced the greatest natural disaster in Ohio history. In March of that year, a series of severe winter rainstorms hit the Midwest. Within three days, 8–11 inches of rain fell throughout the Great Miami River watershed on already saturated soil, resulting in more than 90 percent runoff. The river and its tributaries overflowed. The existing levees failed, and downtown Dayton was flooded up to 20 feet deep. By comparison, the volume of water that passed through the river channel during this storm equals the monthly flow over Niagara Falls. Approximately $100 million worth of property was damaged and 360 lives were lost.

The people of Dayton were determined to prevent a flood like that from ever happening again. The governor appointed people to the Dayton Citizens Relief Commission, and in May 1913, the commission conducted a 10-day fundraiser, collecting more than $2 million (in 1913 dollars) to fund the flood control effort. The result was the construction of the Miami Conservancy District's flood control system, which has prevented flooding in this area more than 1,500 times since its completion.[43]

When water has no place to go, it can be destructive. It continues to accumulate and rise, and with nowhere to go, it floods homes and businesses and can take lives. But water can also be life-giving. When it is allowed to overflow and run off as it goes, water can provide nutrients for growing crops, feeding livestock, and producing life and fruit. Water needs to overflow in healthy ways.

Our money is much the same. Just as a lot of water can be used to produce life or destroy it, so can money. When money is worshiped it becomes blocked up and hoarded, resulting in greed. But when we allow it to overflow where it is needed, the result of that generosity is fruit and life and growth. When money is not allowed to go anywhere, it can result in damage to our own hearts and a withholding of blessing from others. The amazing thing is when money is

---

[43] "The Great 1913 Flood Exhibit," Dayton History, (Carillon Historical Park, June 20, 2016), https://www.daytonhistory.org/visit/things-to-see-do/the-great-1913-flood-exhibit/.

allowed to overflow in healthy ways, just like flood waters, there is always more than enough.

In 2 Corinthians 9:6-15, Paul is writing to the church in Corinth to encourage them to give generously as they have promised. Paul then sends Titus and several others to collect their offering for those in need, saying:

> *Remember this: Whoever sows sparingly will also reap sparingly, and whoever sows generously will also reap generously. Each of you should give what you have decided in your heart to give, not reluctantly or under compulsion, for God loves a cheerful giver. And God is able to bless you abundantly, so that in all things at all times, having all that you need, you will abound in every good work. As it is written: "They have freely scattered their gifts to the poor; their righteousness endures forever."*
>
> *Now he who supplies seed to the sower and bread for food will also supply and increase your store of seed and will enlarge the harvest of your righteousness. You will be enriched in every way so that you can be generous on every occasion, and through us your generosity will result in thanksgiving to God.*
>
> *This service that you perform is not only supplying the needs of the Lord's people but is also overflowing in many expressions of thanks to God. Because of the service by which you have proved yourselves, others will praise God for the obedience that accompanies your confession of the gospel of Christ, and for your generosity in sharing with them and with everyone else. And in their prayers for you their hearts will go out to you, because of the surpassing grace God has given you. Thanks be to God for his indescribable gift!*

In Luke 6:38, Jesus gives a similar message about overflowing generosity. He says:

> *Give, and it will be given to you. A good measure, pressed down, shaken together and running over, will be poured into your lap. For with the measure you use, it will be measured to you.*

If you want to worship God instead of money and enter into this journey of overflowing generosity, the best place to start is with gratitude. You have to let gratitude well up in your heart.

Imagine those spring rains coming down to create the great Dayton flood. The water started to rise. We must let gratitude well up in our hearts in much the same way.

It's so easy to complain. Nothing is ever perfect, but you can choose to look at the positive or the negative, because nothing is ever completely miserable, either. There is always something good, if you look. We can complain about our job, or lack thereof, our spouse, our singleness, our kids, our parents, our neighbors, the weather, our health, the food, the mess, chores, homework, delays, things that break, things we wish we had, the economy, the government, the world … the list goes on and on. It's not hard to look around and see things that could be better. But when we do, we start feeling sorry for ourselves, and the last thing on our minds is being generous. Instead we're thinking, *someone should be generous to us!*

Does this ever happen to you? Your loved ones get on

your nerves so you start to resent them, even though you could not imagine life without them. Your house, car, or possessions need repairs, so you complain, even though you know you are blessed to have those things when so many people in the world live on next to nothing. We can quickly forget the blessings in our lives.

That's why gratitude is so powerful. It breaks the power of negativity and selfishness. It stops the downward spiral and starts to lift you up. Gratitude is a form of worshiping God. Focusing on our stuff, or the lack thereof, is also a form of worship—a form of worshiping material wealth.

Giving thanks can fill you up with joy and gratitude. So, when you are feeling ungrateful, it's time to break through with gratitude.

Remember that 2 Corinthians 9:8 says:

> *And God is able to bless you abundantly, so that in all things at all times, having all that you need, you will abound in every good work.*

Where has God blessed you abundantly? Where has God given you all that you need?

Start a practice of giving thanks. It can be a written list when you notice yourself focusing inward, on your own wants and needs. It can be a spoken list as you drift off to sleep at the end of a long day. It can be part of a spiritual practice of journaling. Or it can be something you do with loved ones around a dining room table.

Thank God for your job and His financial provision, for a season of transition if you are in-between work, for the things you love about your spouse, for the joys of singleness, for your kids, your parents, your neighbors, for the weather (even the cold, the heat, or the endless days of rain), your health, the food God has provided, the things you are blessed to have even when it results in more mess to clean up, for household chores that mean you have a roof over your head, for homework and the ability to learn, for delays that give you the opportunity to pause, the economy, the government, for the world that God so loved …

The more you give thanks, the more life doesn't seem so bad. As Julie Andrews sings in *The Sound of Music*:

When the dog bites,
When the bee stings,
When I'm feeling sad,
I simply remember my favorite things,
And then I don't feel so bad.[44]

Take a minute and write down five things you are grateful for today. No, really. Stop reading and list out five blessings. This is your gratitude break.

---

[44] *The Sound of Music, The Sound of Music* (IMBD), accessed September 4, 2020, https://www.imdb.com/title/tt0059742/.

1.

2.

3.

4.

5.

***

God has blessed each of us abundantly and supplied our needs. Do not be an ungrateful recipient. If we are going to overflow with generosity, we have to start with giving thanks. Next, we give God our trust.

Giving is a major act of trust. It is saying, *God, I trust you more than the amount of money in my bank account.* It's saying, *I am going to put you first Lord, and trust you for my needs, and that is scary.* Many Christians say "Yes" to trusting Jesus Christ in every area of their lives, except with their money. It's like this final holdout. *God, I trust you as my Lord and Savior, but I need to keep control of my money.* It's one of the most common areas where we try to hold back. However, if we can trust God as our Savior, if we believe God is good and faithful and true, then we can trust God when He says giving is good.

If you don't take our word for it, God invites you to test Him in this one area. It's the only area we see God inviting us to test Him to see if His word is true. Malachi 3:10 says, "'Bring the whole tithe into the storehouse, that there may be food in my house. Test me in this,' says the Lord Almighty, 'and see if I will not throw open the floodgates of heaven and pour out so much blessing that there will not be room enough to store it.'"

A tithe simply means one tenth. It's also to be the first one tenth that is set apart, belonging to God. It is about putting God first. We worship God with our first and our best and trust Him to bless the rest!

When Callie was a child, her parents taught her this principle of tithing. You can start it at any age, but the sooner you start, the easier it is to make it a habit. She started receiving an allowance for helping around the house, but to ensure that having exact change would never be an excuse to not tithe, Callie's parents always made sure part of her allowance was in coins. If her allowance was

$3.00, the last dollar was in coins so that she could put 30 cents in the offering plate at church. Now, sometimes that 30 cents ended up being used at the donut table at church, but it was still going back to God's work, and that practice of tithing stuck early.

As Callie got older, her tithing evolved. When she began babysitting and earning more income, she tithed 10 percent on whatever she received. When she had summer jobs in high school and college, she tithed. When she got her first post-college job, Callie started working in investment banking and had so much fun because now 10 percent was an even bigger amount to give. Right out of college, Callie was giving more than adults who were much older and wealthier, but it was because she was tithing, not simply because she was making more. Tithing gave her some exciting opportunities, too. The church's women's ministry needed a computer, so she gave to meet that need. Friends who graduated with Callie from college became missionaries, and she was able to be one of their supporters. Because she was prioritizing giving and setting aside a tithe, Callie had money to give and could joyfully respond as needs emerged. The more you experience the joy of generosity, the more you freely give, the easier it is to part with money, and the temptation to worship money loses its power.

Roz's tithing journey looked a bit different than Callie's. Roz's immediate family immigrated from Sicily to the United States in the late 1970's. Sicily is an island off the coast of Italy, but has remained a culture set apart from its mainland counterpart. Sicily has a rich history. However, the area is still developing and wrestles with poverty even today. Roz's parents barely had a middle school education. They also did not speak English when they made the journey to America. Roz was raised in a meager household without extravagant resources. When Roz decided he would be the first in his family to go to college, his parents didn't have the financial resources to pay for school. Roz scraped by working jobs and enlisting in the Marine Corps Reserves. While that helped alleviate some financial pressures, Roz still had to take out loans to pay for college and then seminary. When Roz was starting in ministry, he was not making a large salary, but he had a passion for paying off the $60,000 he had accumulated in student loan debt. As Roz was paying off the debt, he was tempted to neglect tithing. However, Roz was aggressive in saving the extra money he received from birthdays, holidays, and other special occasions to pay down his debt, and God challenged him to continue to tithe in the midst of it all.

Roz chose to honor God with his giving, even though it didn't make sense from the world's vantage point. Roz was obedient, and three years later, he became debt-free while still giving his tithe to the Lord. Roz became convinced that besides self-discipline, his offering to God blessed him with the ability to get out of debt. Later, when God was calling Roz to pursue a doctoral degree, we decided that the only way he would go back to school was if God supplied the money. The first school Roz applied to was a program that was going to give him a full scholarship. However, after much prayer and discernment, Roz declined the offer because he felt that the Lord was directing him to attend a different seminary—one that couldn't offer much in scholarship money. After Roz was accepted to this second seminary, his colleagues told him that he was crazy for turning down the first school. But then a miracle happened that Roz would never forget. The seminary did something they don't typically do: they gave Roz a full scholarship! It's amazing how God blesses us in tangible and intangible ways to meet the pressing needs in front of us. Today, Roz shares his story with recent graduates and congregations. People often think they will give back to God when they get out of debt or make more money. However, if the discipline is not started immediately in one's discipleship journey, it will not happen on its own or by accident. Giving has to be an intentional effort of trusting that God will provide.

Here's another giving story from our friend Pastor Joshua Clough. He wrote this on Facebook:

> *Growing up my dad taught me to give 10% of my mowing money. Tough lesson for a kid. I graduated college, then seminary and didn't have a lot, so I never thought much about giving, unfortunately. I started pastoring and had significant student loans. I knew deep down I needed to tithe but lived in fear because of student loans. That started to change when Claire and I married. I felt compelled, impressed upon by God that I needed to start tithing. I was convicted. So, we started to give 10% first. No matter*

what. There were some really hard months in San Diego. Then, I took a pay cut to come to the staff of Church of the Resurrection (COR) in Leawood, KS. I saw that move as being faithful, and we were still tithing. We started to chip away at those loans, using the Dave Ramsey snowball method. My truck was falling apart but then a grandmother provided us a new truck. We sold the old one and paid off another loan. Both of us (Claire works at COR too) received a raise which enabled us to pay more loans off. We launched a new church here. I just finished my doctoral degree and was awarded another raise. We saw all these as God's provision and blessing. But, if we hadn't made the plan to tithe and pay off debt, we would not have been able to fully receive the blessing. I don't subscribe to a prosperity theology, but I do believe God asks us to be faithful to what He gives, and when we are, we find abundant blessing. Through all this we've become more generous and able to give more. Amazingly, in about two and a quarter years, we paid off $110,000 of student loans. I share this story with other young couples who feel burdened and saddled by student debt. We just paid our last loan payment in August!"

Tithing teaches us to prioritize our life around God, the One we really want to worship. It teaches an abundance mindset that the Macedonian churches had. It builds our faith in God's faithfulness. We have never met anyone who regretted tithing. Maybe some regretted where they gave if they found out the gift was not appreciated or used wisely, but no one we've met has ever regretted the practice. Here's the crazy part about giving: We think we will miss out, on our goals or life experiences in general, but when we partner with God in joyful obedience, somehow it works. That is where the Malachi 3:10 challenge to test God comes in. We invite you to try it, even for a season. Try tithing 10 percent for the next 12 months and see if you can make your budget work. See what happens when you put God first and give Him your trust.

* * *

The next thing that happens when you let gratitude fill up your life is you begin to open your heart to be generous in all areas.

When the waters rise up due to heavy rain, you must give them a place to go. After the great Dayton flood, the city put in a flood control system to release the waters into various areas that could use the water. As our hearts start to well up with gratitude, it is time to let them overflow in generosity around you. Money hoarded turns into destructive greed and causes damage much like a flood. That is why we cannot worship money. When we share our financial blessings, our generosity overflows and blesses others who can in turn bless others. Remember:

> *And God is able to bless you abundantly, so that in all things at all times, having all that you need, you will* ***abound*** *in every good work.*
>
> **2 Corinthians 9:8**

God does not bless you so that you can hoard those blessings. He blesses you so that out of the abundance can come good work.

"Give, and it will be given to you. A good measure, pressed down, shaken together and running over, will be poured into your lap. For with the measure you use, it will be measured to you" (Luke 6:38). This is overflowing generosity.

As you give it a place to go, it's important to plan your generosity. Without a plan, good intentions fall flat. In 2 Corinthians 9, Paul is writing to the Corinthian church about the Macedonians, wanting the Corinthians to be inspired and ready. You see, the Corinthians had already said they were going to give, and it was in part their commitment to give that had inspired the Macedonians to give so generously. Now, Paul's colleague Titus and several others were coming to collect the offering, and Paul did not want them to get there and the Corinthians to have failed to plan for the generous gift they promised. "You see, I wanted to give but… I guess I ate out a few too many times… there was this sale I couldn't pass up… the car battery needed replacing…" The Corinthians' excuses probably looked a little different than these ones that we have today, but Paul knew their excuses would come up. That is why he writes:

> *So I thought it necessary to urge the brothers to visit you in advance and finish the arrangements for the generous gift you had promised. Then it will be ready as a generous gift, not as one grudgingly given."*
>
> **2 Corinthians 9:5**

When we make a plan, we can give generously with joy. When we do not plan, that is when our commitments feel like a weight. Giving is good. It is meant to be fun. That is why it is important to plan.

One of Callie's passions when she has the time is financial coaching. She was meeting with a couple who really wanted to tithe. They knew God's Word, but they did not know if they could hit that 10 percent goal. The couple had done Dave Ramsey's Financial Peace University. They had gone through the Crown Financial Ministries course. The problem was they had never really stopped to make a budget, so giving never happened, and their spending got out of control. Callie sat down with the couple and helped them make a budget, the tithe coming out first. Then, she worked with them to create a plan to save, pay off debt, and take care of the rest of their bills with the other 90 percent of their budget. If we do not plan, it does not happen.

Once you have a budget, automate the important parts of your plan. Set your giving to come out of your paycheck first, followed by saving and essential living expenses. When you make your priorities the priority, your life stays in order. When you are not intentional, your best intentions do not come to fruition.

In 2019, we experimented with not automating our giving. Some of our income became more sporadic, so we thought we would just give every few months and keep track. Bad idea. Why? Because life happens. We kept getting behind, and then it was harder to catch up. That is why it is a first fruits principle. Set it up to happen automatically, whether that is monthly, weekly, bi-weekly, or as soon as you get paid if your income fluctuates. When you have a plan and you automate it, you can be generous, and it takes the burden out of being generous.

Make a decision right now. If you are not tithing yet, begin somewhere. Pick a percentage of your income to give and set it up to happen automatically. If you are not ready for 10 percent, don't let that stop you. Start somewhere. Commit to it for a year, and then see if you can grow it next year. If you grow it 1 percent every year, soon you will be at 10 percent or even higher.

If you were giving, but not tithing 10 percent yet, can you grow your giving? Look at what you gave last year, and figure out what percentage that is of your income, and increase it. The beauty of a percentage is the amount fluctuates with your income. As God blesses you, you will have more to give.

Want to really have some fun? Are you ready to test God and tithe 10 percent? We cannot wait to hear your testimony of what God does in and through you as a result. You are about to see God move in your life through joyful obedience, both as you experience the blessing of giving and as you see God guide you as you stretch the rest.

How about something even crazier? Second Corinthians 9:7 says, "Each of you should give what you have decided in your heart to give, not reluctantly or under compulsion, for God loves a cheerful giver."

The translation here of "cheerful" comes from the Greek word *hilaron*, which comes from the same root *hileos*, from which we get the word "hilarious." Are you ready for some laugh-out-loud, joy-filled, hilarious giving? Maybe you have been tithing for a while, but is God calling you to try more?

Other Christians might think you are crazy. The world will think you are ridiculous. But, what if? What if you tried it? Can you grow the percentage you give beyond 10 percent? Maybe you start doing a special Christmas gift each year above and beyond your regular giving, putting your church and favorite ministries on your list along with family and friends who get Christmas gifts. Could you build in non-tax-deductible giving to bless individuals in need? If you have kids, you could get them involved in some top-secret, anonymous giving missions to teach them the joy of giving while they are still young. Another idea is to gather some friends and start a giving circle.

Commit to a certain amount you put into the pool each month and then choose a charity or individuals to bless. If you will be giving to churches or non-profit organizations, a donor advised fund, offered by organizations like National Christian Foundation and local community foundations, is a great way to pool your giving in an easy and organized way, plus you get a tax receipt.

The options are endless when you start getting creative with God. Pray and talk to your spouse or anyone you partner with in your giving.

Then, the important thing is to start being generous *now*. Callie is a planner, and knowingly admits she can wait and wait and keep tweaking her plan to get it just perfect. Maybe you are a planner as well. You want to figure things out perfectly, but then you never get around to starting. Life is busy, so this can happen easily. But if you never start, you don't get anywhere. It is time to start being generous now.

Pray about your generosity, make a plan, but then put it into action. If you are worried your plan is not perfect, it's not. Our plans never are, but when we start, God will guide us and help us adjust along the way.

Paul goes on to tell the Corinthian:

> *Each of you should give what you have decided in your heart to give, not reluctantly or under compulsion, for God loves a cheerful giver. And God is able to bless you abundantly, so that in all things at all times, having all that you need, you will* ***abound*** *in every good work.*
>
> **2 Corinthians 9: 7-8**

God loves you! God loves you so much! And God would not tell you to give to hurt you. God wants to bless you abundantly, to grow your faith, so that in all things, at all times, having all that you need, you will abound in every good work.

Giving is good! Giving is fun! Remember that the word for cheerful in 2 Corinthians 9:7 is translated as hilarious. Giving should bring you so much joy that you are filled with laughter. So, whatever you have decided in your heart to give, do it. Give it a try. Test God and watch the fun begin.

God does not need your money. God could make money rain down from Heaven to take care of the needs of others, but instead He chooses to use you. Why? Because God wants your heart, and where your treasure is, there your heart will be also. As we give, we not only experience the joy of being used by God to bless others, but giving also results in thanksgiving.

Second Corinthians 9:11-13 says:

> *You will be enriched in every way so that you can be generous on every occasion, and through us your generosity will result in* ***thanksgiving*** *to God. This service that you perform is not only supplying the needs of the Lord's people but is also* ***overflowing*** *in many expressions of thanks to God. Because of the service by which you have proved yourselves,* ***others will praise*** *God for the obedience that accompanies your confession of the gospel of Christ, and for your generosity in sharing with them and with everyone else.*

Giving doesn't make sense. Why would you give to someone else what you could keep for yourself? But we know the joy giving produces when we see God take our giving and blessing others.

When giving becomes a part of your lifestyle, the impact is tremendous. An often-overlooked disciple, Tabitha, also known as Dorcas in the Greek, lived in Joppa. Acts 9:36 tells us, "She was always doing good and helping the poor." That was Dorcas's reputation. Then, she became sick and died. Her impact had been so tremendous that when people heard that Peter was in a town nearby, they went and found him and urged him to come at once. When he arrived, the widows stood around crying and showing Peter all of the clothes Dorcas had made for them. Dorcas lived out the "pure religion" James talked about in James 1:27, looking after widows through her generosity.

Dorcas's generosity had impacted so many that the people she served found Peter, who prayed for Dorcas's healing even though she was already dead. Then, a miracle happened, and God brought Dorcas back to life. As word spread, so did revival, and many people came to believe in Jesus Christ as their Lord because of this event (Acts 9:36-42).

The impact did not stop there, though. In the 1800's, a charitable movement of Dorcas Societies began and spread all over the world. Inspired by Dorcas the disciple, these groups followed her example of providing clothing and other physical needs to the poor.[45] Who will your generosity inspire?

The world would have us squander our money, to waste it on things that do not matter in the long run—to accumulate fancy new stuff that does not ever make us happy like the ads said it will. Giving is equally as lavish. Why would you just give away hard-earned money? Why would you give it to someone who didn't do anything to earn it? Who didn't work for it? It's your money after all. You should do something for *you* with it.

---

45 "All the Women of the Bible – Dorcas." BibleGateway https://www.biblegateway.com/resources/all-women-bible/Dorcas

When we give generously as God leads us, it often looks like the woman who came to Jesus when he was in Bethany at the home of Simon the Leper (Matthew 26:6-13). This woman came with an alabaster jar of very expensive perfume and poured it on Jesus's head, anointing him. Consider the response of Jesus's disciples: "When the disciples saw this, they were indignant. 'Why this waste?' they asked" (Matthew 26:8).

Often, even fellow believers will see our generosity and question it. Jesus defends this woman and honors her gift. Are you going to squander your money on things that do not matter, or are you going to lavishly give it to glorify the One who gave it to you in the first place? We want to invite you into some "wasteful" giving.

Part of "wasteful" giving involves trusting God with how the money is used once it's given. That means the recipient may or may not use it exactly as you would like, but that is between them and God. Would you be okay with that?

Now, if you are a recipient of generosity, we are not saying you should ignore donor intent. Callie has been working in fundraising for more than a dozen years, and always encourages organizations to honor the wishes of the person making a gift. If you cannot fulfill those original wishes, that is an opportunity for a conversation. Is there another option that works for the donor and the organization? If the donor is unwilling to bend their expectations, the organization then is faced with a hard decision to either refuse or return the gift. There are often donors with something very specific they want to give to, and sometimes it is God-led and aligns with the organization's mission, and that is fine. In other cases, that intent can cross the line into control. On the opposite end, there are generous givers out there who trust the organization and release the money once the gift is made.

One of the most generous couples Callie has worked with in her role at United Theological Seminary embodies this open-handed generosity. While Callie and the leaders of United always update the donors on any possible change to the way their funds might be used, this couple's constant response is, "That is fine. However, you need to use the funds. When we give a gift, it is yours to use as you see fit." They so personify this heart of generosity that when they issued a matching gift challenge to encourage others in giving, this couple was quick to say, "This money is not from us. We see everything we have as a gift from God, so this is simply us passing along what God has given to us."

When God puts it on your heart to give, do you release the money or keep strings attached to it? When you give, do you need the recognition, or do you want God to get the credit?

We have talked with people that want their gift to be completely anonymous so that they are not tempted to boast. They know their own heart, and often draw on Matthew 6:1-4 to "not let your left hand know what your right hand is doing" when it comes to giving.

Others use their giving as a platform to give God the glory and encourage others to give. Both are valid, and there may be times you do one or the other depending on the size of the gift, relationship with the organization, or because of something in your own heart. Let God lead you, not just in what you give, but also in how you do it.

If you want to give anonymously and also receive a tax deduction, most organizations will honor that request, though someone at the organization will then know you gave. If you want to give without anyone at the recipient organization knowing you gave the gift, a donor advised fund is a great solution. Callie worked for National Christian Foundation, which is the largest Christian provider of donor advised funds. When you make a gift into the donor advised fund, you receive your tax deduction. Then, you can request grants be sent to recipient organizations whenever you are ready, and you can choose to have the gift sent anonymously. Because your tax deduction came from the organization where you have a fund, the ultimate beneficiary would only know the gift came from that foundation and not you specifically, if you choose the anonymous option. A donor advised fund is also a great tool for tax planning, especially if you do a significant amount of giving.

Giving draws you closer to the heart of God. God is the generous giver of life, beauty, creation, provision, and ultimately salvation. "For God so loved the world that He gave His only son…" (John 3:16). God in His very nature and core is generous. When we give, it reflects God's image, and points others to Him.

Has the Lord ever called you to give a sacrificial gift? Would your heart be open to that? While giving should be a regular habit in all our lives as followers of Jesus, there are times where God will call you to give above and beyond. If you truly trust and believe that everything belongs to the Lord, then your open hands will allow God to direct you in lavish, "wasteful" ways of giving. It may be one of the scariest, most fun things you ever do, when you so clearly hear God saying this is what I want you to give and you faithfully give in response.

Our friend Rev. Wayne Botkin says, "If the Lord gives you a vision, the Lord will make the provision." Abraham was willing to sacrifice his son Isaac on the altar in obedience to God, and God provided a ram (Genesis 22). In the same way, when God calls us to make a gift so sacrificial that we have no idea how we will be able to do it, yet we trust God, He will provide.

One of our friends, Sungkyoon Park, is a Korean student at United Theological Seminary. Sungkyoon is one of the most prayerful, gentle, and generous human beings one could ever encounter. At one point, Sungkyoon decided to start a prayer group that quickly multiplied from one gathering to five gatherings a week. On top of that, Sungkyoon also attends his local church every morning at

6:00 am for corporate prayer. Sungkyoon's intimacy with God has softened his ears to hear God's direction for his life and the needs of others. Behind the scenes, Sungkyoon would quietly raise scholarship and tuition money for his fellow international students. Whenever he would hear about a need, he would pray, contribute his limited resources, and ask God to provide the rest. In the world's eyes, it would not make much sense for Sungkyoon to give money away sacrificially that he could use for himself. However, Sungkyoon continually sacrifices his own time and limited resources to help struggling international students navigating how to pay for theological education. It's no surprise that since Sungkyoon became part of the seminary community he has raised and given away thousands of dollars in scholarship money and aid for others over the course of a few years. All of this was done quietly and behind the scenes, out of the public eye.

When it comes to giving when you're married, as in all areas of finance, it is important to be on the same page with your spouse. Money can be a major source of tension in so many relationships, but if you are both seeking God and praying, God will guide you. Even if only one of the spouses is a Christian, God can use that spouse's prayers. The area Roz and I seem to fight most about in our marriage is giving, in part because we both love to give but are wired very differently. Callie is a planner and likes to stick to a plan once it has been made. Roz loves spontaneous giving.

If he feels an urge to give, he wants to give right then and there. Both are good. Callie's planning helps Roz be intentional with his giving. Roz's spontaneity keeps Callie more open to the Spirit's leading with generosity. We now plan for spontaneous giving. That might sound crazy, but knowing God is going to move and bring forward new giving opportunities, we intentionally set money aside to respond to those as they arise. God did not give you a spouse to frustrate you. He gave you your spouse to bless you. How might God use the way your spouse is wired to help you grow in your journey of generosity?

Another area God has been growing us, and Callie especially, is in setting aside funds for non-tax-deductible giving. This is not as big of an issue for many now that the standard deduction has been raised, but it is still a budgeting issue. Often the needs of individuals arise that cannot be fulfilled through a non-profit organization. We wanted to be flexible to respond to those, so we set some money aside each year to bless others. This is where being open-handed with giving can really come into play. If you choose to bless someone you know, it can easily change the nature of the relationship if you are not careful. If it is truly a gift, then they do not owe you anything and should be trusted to use the gift however they want, even if it does not align with your original intentions. Now, you might choose not to give them a future gift as a result, but how they use what has been given is between that person and the Lord.

Anonymous giving can also be helpful here.

In this same vein, we also choose to avoid lending money to friends and family. Proverbs 22:7 reminds us that "the borrower is slave to the lender." Lending money changes the nature of the relationship. Normally, we decide instead if we would be willing to simply give them money instead of lend it. If that person wants to repay us, we often insist that they pay it forward to bless someone else instead. In the rare case where we do lend money, in our hearts and minds we consider the money lent a gift. If the recipient does repay it, great. If not, we make sure we are okay with it becoming a gift.

Generosity also extends beyond dollars and cents to stuff. If everything you own belongs to the Lord, God should have access to all of it. Here are just a few giving examples to hopefully get your mind turning and your heart open.

One of the things we have been blessed with at different points in our lives has been a home with extra space. This has given us the opportunity to host people in our home for meals who might not ever be able to reciprocate the offer. One tradition we started when we lived in Lexington was having people over for Christmas Day brunch. We invited friends who did not have family in town that we knew might not have anyone to celebrate Christmas with. One friend years later continues to thank us—that simple gesture touched him so deeply in the middle of a hard year in his life.

In addition, we've often had extra bedrooms in our

homes, which has given us the opportunity to offer space to a variety of people: out of town seminary students in town for an intensive, a family moving who needed a few months to sell their previous house before they could afford housing in Dayton, friends who were homeless and needed a place other than a shelter to live, and friends in ministry who were not making big salaries but having big Kingdom impact. Having someone live with you longer term can grow and stretch you, especially if you are used to having your own space, but in each case, we were so richly blessed by the people we shared life with in that season.

So often, being generous blesses the giver. As Jesus himself shared, "It is more blessed to give than to receive" (Acts 20:35).

Sometimes the item you give is smaller, but the action has a big impact in your heart. People often give away old clothes that they do not wear, sometimes in good condition, but other times with stains and worn out. Rarely do we give away items that we still love to wear. Callie was at an Election Day communion service one February, and the church was doing a coat drive. Callie had come from the gym and was wearing her favorite University of Kentucky sweatshirt. She felt God's clear yet gentle nudge to part with that beloved sweatshirt. A little sheepish because she was literally taking off the item she was wearing, Callie added that bright blue sweatshirt to the pile with a prayer that it would bless its new owner. She, of course, had other warm clothes at home, but the impact of her obedience to God's prompting brought Callie a joy that is hard to explain.

When God says something and you eventually do it, the most refreshing and awesome sense of freedom and joy bursts into your life. Once we finally get to that act of obedience, we think, *Why did I wait?* There is so much freedom in doing what God says.

Roz had a similar experience one winter. One of the folks at Mosaic Church started a ministry near and dear to his heart. This man and another friend would go out to a certain area of Dayton where there was a camp for those without homes. It is a community of people who made the decision to sleep and live outside for a variety of reasons. The Mosaic servants would go out there, build relationships, share their stories, and, when applicable, provide for some physical needs. One afternoon Roz decided to go out to the camp with them. They enjoyed a meal and were talking about faith. Roz asked one of the guys who lived there what some of his needs were. The man mentioned that he needed a new pair of shoes. The pair he was wearing was literally falling off his feet. Roz asked him what size he needed. He told Roz size 8, which was Roz's exact shoe size. Then Roz felt something inside of him say, *Give this man your shoes.* At first, Roz tried to rationalize it in his head and negotiate that he did not have enough time to run home and get a pair of shoes and come back. Then the feeling grew stronger, and God said, *Give him the shoes you are wearing right now.*

So, Roz asked the guy if he would like to try on his shoes. The man obliged, and they fit perfectly. That day, Roz came home wearing a worn-out pair of falling apart shoes and a heart filled with joy and gratitude.

The next week during worship at Mosaic, Roz was waiting to get up to preach and in walked the same gentleman he gave the shoes to. When Roz looked down at his feet, he noticed the man was wearing the shoes. We hope that act of obedience blessed the recipient, but boy, did it bless Roz!

There are instances when we can hear God's voice clearly through Scripture, a feeling, a picture, or an impression. The feeling Roz got that day at the camp was so overwhelming that he knew he needed to act right away. There are many times it is easy for us to ignore that voice, but there are other times it is so clear that we must act.

We live in an age overrun with ever-improving technology, and it seems impossible to keep up. Things change every few months, and consumers have become hooked on technology like a drug. If you want evidence of this, walk into any Apple store around the time a new Apple device like the latest iPhone becomes available on the market—lines overcrowd the store and spill out onto the sidewalks. This kind of frenzy prepares folks for Christmas shopping, as malls across America experience a flood of shoppers for Black Friday, Brown Thursday (also known as Thanksgiving), and all the days leading up to December

25th. As if grown-up toys and gadgets were not fun enough already, the toys that kids have nowadays are far superior to Roz's GI Joe and He-Man figures of the 1980's. When Roz was a kid, his favorite part of getting new toys was the first few days playing with them, until he got bored with the toys or broke them.

At one of our churches a few years ago, we encountered a young girl named Syd. Syd was like every kid who enjoys games, fun, and toys, but she had this propensity for giving and sharing her toys at a remarkably young age. Syd is an example of what generosity looks like, even on her birthday of all days! Syd's birthday falls a few weeks before Christmas, so she began a tradition of asking friends to bring a gift not for her, but for someone in need instead. Then, she gives all of these birthday gifts away to children in the Dayton community who desire to have wrapped presents under their tree. Syd had done this for a number of years; the last official count was at least five straight years. Syd's generosity embodies the words of Jesus in Matthew 18:3, "unless you change and become like little children, you will never enter the kingdom of heaven." Syd does not give to brag or receive accolades, but simply to put others above herself. Holiday shopping and spending can become burdensome, but how can Christ followers reclaim the meaning of Christmas and make a positive impact on the lives of those around us?

Another fun Christmas tradition to try is joining the

Giving Tuesday movement. Giving Tuesday started in 2012 as a simple way to encourage generosity. We already had Black Friday, Small Business Saturday, and Cyber Monday, so why not Giving Tuesday? Celebrated annually on the Tuesday after Thanksgiving, Giving Tuesday has become a global movement. You can give to any church, charity, or cause you like, the idea is simply to set aside a day to give intentionally and encourage others to be generous.

***

If you want to be more generous, you must make it a priority. Start with giving. Give lavishly and abundantly and cheerfully in whatever amount God puts on your heart. Pick a percentage of your income and faithfully start there, but then see if you can grow it a little every year. Maybe you're not tithing 10 percent yet because you are not sure where the money will come from. As it stands, there is already more month than money. Start somewhere. Maybe it is 3 percent, but next year, you increase your giving to 4 percent, then 5, then 6, then 7, and before you know it you are tithing, and the remainder of your money is stretching to cover the rest.

Do not wait until you have more money. The more you make, the harder that money becomes to part with. If you start giving a percentage of your income now, as your income grows, so will your giving, and you will not miss that extra money.

On the other hand, maybe God's calling you to step out in faith and start giving 10 percent right now. You have never done that before, but in order to trust God with your finances, you want to start with giving back to advance God's Kingdom first. We are so excited for you! You are about to go on a God-adventure that will stretch you spiritually and grow your faith.

Maybe you have been tithing for so long, it is almost automatic. Right now, spend some time asking God what He would have you do. Does God want you to give more in this season? Is it a one-time gift, a percentage increase, or a commitment of extra resources as they come in through odd jobs, tax returns, a garage sale, or birthday gifts? Let God lead you and guide you.

This is not what God is going to call everyone to do, but just to stretch your giving imagination—especially if God's blessed you with significant financial resources—what would it look like to reverse tithe? Rick Warren, founding pastor of Saddleback Valley Community Church in Southern California and author of *The Purpose Driven Life*, among other books, began his marriage with his wife Kay tithing 10 percent. But they did not stop there. Instead, Rick and Kay kept increasing their giving by 1 percent or more every year.[46] By the time they had been married 32 years, they were giving 90 percent of their income away and living on

---

46 Barbara Bradley Hagerty, "Rick Warren: The Purpose-Driven Pastor," NPR (NPR, January 18, 2009), https://www.npr.org/templates/story/story.php?storyId=99529977.

10 percent, also known as a reverse tithe.[47] God had blessed them financially, and they experienced the incredible joy of blessing others. Do not let your giving become legalistic, but boldly give whatever the Lord places on your heart to give, even if it sounds ridiculous.

If your money speaks a lot about what you value and worship, where do your credit card and bank statements say you are squandering your money? Where is it being wasted, a few dollars here and a few dollars there? Where is your money being spent worshiping other things or hoarded to worship money itself?

Every financial decision is a lifestyle decision, and most lifestyle decisions have financial implications. If you are going to cut back on your finances, a good starting place is to think about the life you live and what you love.

Take out a piece of paper or open a new note on your smartphone. Start by listing your top five priorities in life. This can include relationships that are important to you, things you love doing, and things or activities you are passionate about.

Next, take a look at your checkbook and/or most recent credit card statement. What expenses line up with your priorities? Where are you spending money on things that are not important to you at all? How can you cut out or cut back on things that are not important to you?

---

47 "What is a Reverse Tithe?" https://bigthink.com/videos/what-is-a-reverse-tithe

Did you list spending quality time with your family, yet you spend over $100/month on cable TV, satellite, or premium stations that keep you from spending real quality time with your family? Do you claim that you would be happy living a less expensive lifestyle, yet you spent more than 40 percent of your income on a nicer home or apartment? Cutting back on the things that are not priorities, or are contrary to your priorities, will help you live a life focused on what is important to you, and help you save money at the same time.

What if your spending does line up with your priorities? Are there lifestyle changes you can make to decrease your spending in a particular category? Rather than cut out a category completely, can you step down to a less expensive alternative?

A friend named Sarah was talking with some other friends about getting fit together. They talked about joining a gym together or signing up for dance classes, but knowing none of them had a lot of extra cash to spend, Sarah suggested starting a walking group. They meet weekly to walk together and get the accountability for working out, but it was a less expensive alternative to paying for a gym membership or class.

A few years ago, Callie recognized that she was spending a large amount of money going out with friends. She realized if she switched to drinking water rather than ordering a beverage that cost money, she was still able to spend time with them, but that simple lifestyle change shaved dollars off her budget daily.

If you are spending a lot of money on clothes, and shopping is not an idol, can you step down from expensive department stores and designer shops to mid-priced department stores or outlets? If you are already at mid-priced department stores and outlets, what about stepping down to discount stores or consignment stores? If you already shop there, what about trying thrift stores or hand me downs?

If you can cut out excessive spending in the areas that are not important to you or step down to less expensive options, those small lifestyle changes can add up weekly and monthly to big savings. Pick at least one item to cut out, cut back on, or switch to a less expensive alternative this year. Would you even miss it?

If you are worried you would miss it too much, or the change seems too hard, try the switch only for a set time period. Perhaps it is a 40 day fast over Lent or during Advent and you take the money you would have spent and give it instead to a cause you care about. Maybe it is a commitment for a semester if you are in school, or for a year if you are extra brave. Pick the change you are making, the timeframe, and where that money will go instead.

Callie was leading a bible study that met weekly at Starbucks, when one of the women in the group pointed out how much they were collectively spending on coffee. They decided to make a change, and started meeting at our house for a cup of coffee brewed in our coffee pot. They found a jar, and each week contributed what they would have spent on coffee out. At the end of the study, Callie's group went on a canned goods shopping spree to donate to the local food pantry. It was an easy change, but committing to it as a group and knowing what the money was going to made it fun.

One of the women in that bible study was a newer Christian. She had been spending a lot of her money on designer jeans, a brand called "True Religion." God convicted her that those jeans had become an idol. She thought about donating the jeans to Goodwill so that they would not possess her anymore (sometimes our possessions start to possess us, if we cannot bear to give them up). This woman realized that she could bless a lot more people by selling them instead. So that is what she did, parting with her beloved jeans and giving the proceeds to charity.

***

Money speaks so powerfully about what is important, what we worship. If the Kingdom of God is the most important thing in your life, how are you investing to spread the Good News, to care for the least and lost, and to spread love in the name of Jesus? Instead of worshiping money, use your money to worship God.

Giving is an act of worship. That is why it is an important part of worship when Christians gather on Sunday mornings or for worship services during the week. Of course, the church needs money to function, but that should not be the top reason we give, or the main reason the pastor asks people to give. Giving should first and foremost be a way of worshiping God as Lord of your life—a way to love God and love your neighbor. It places our trust in God rather than money. It breaks the bonds greed and materialism try to have on our heart. It frees us to walk in joyful obedience with God.

Too many times pastors and leaders encourage giving from a place of guilt: If you do not give, the church will close. If you do not give, you will not experience God's favor. If you do not give, you are not a good Christian.

Giving should not be from a place of guilt, but from a place of love. The apostle Paul has a lot to say on this topic to the church in Corinth. In 1 Corinthians 13:3 he says, "If I give all I possess to the poor...but do not have love, I gain nothing." Then, in 2 Corinthians 9:7 Paul explains, "Each of you should give what you have decided in your heart to give, not reluctantly or under compulsion, for God loves a cheerful giver." As an individual, is your giving from a place of love for God and love for your neighbor? Is your giving helping you live out that Greatest Commandment? If not, take a moment to explore your motives. Why are you giving? Is it to impress others? Because you feel like you should or have to? Dig a little deeper into those motives to figure out where they came from. It might be how you were raised or the messages you heard from church. What would it take to rearrange your motives, to get back to giving with joy and love?

In other cases, pastors and leaders are reluctant to talk about giving. They are not comfortable with the topic, in part because they have seen it done poorly so many times. Start with your own giving journey. Why do you give? Many people are just as afraid of sharing their faith because they were worried about doing it wrong. Just as there is power in sharing your testimony of accepting Christ as your Lord and Savior, there is power in sharing your giving testimony. Why did you first start giving? How does God use giving in your own life and faith? Why do you give to your church or the ministries you support? No one can deny your own experience, and they can often find themselves in your story. Do not be afraid to share.

If you are a pastor or leader and are not giving generously, it is time to get honest with yourself and explore why. Often, it is because our own finances are not in the best shape. Giving should still be our top priority.

Callie was at the funeral of a very generous woman and the pastor shared how that woman impacted his own giving. She found out he was not tithing, and she simply challenged him to start. He had rationalized in his own mind that he was giving his life to ministry and could make a lot more money in the for-profit world, so that was his justification for not giving. This parishioner simply encouraged him to try. If he expected members of the church to tithe, he needed to set an example with his own life. At the time of the funeral, the pastor had been tithing for years as a result of this woman's gentle urging. Without her encouragement, he would not have started and would have missed out on the blessing. As a result of his own experience of the joy of generosity, he could more confidently invite others to give.

If you are a pastor or Christian leader, the number one reason people do not give is because they are never asked. Too often in church, we simply pass an offering plate and tell people how to give—never saying why and never with an invitation. Simon Sinek has become famous in the business world for his book *Start with Why: How Great Leaders Inspire Everyone to Take Action*. If you start with why, with casting vision, people will be more likely to follow. When you start with what or how, some may join, but the impact will not be the same. People give because they are asked, but also because they believe in the vision and they trust the visionary. If you as a leader are giving and communicating the why powerfully, others are more likely to join you.

Those givers will stay with you if they see the impact of their gift. Keeping the lights on is not impact. Lives changed is impact. How are you as a leader saying thank you and letting people know that their gift mattered? Each event, each person that accepts Christ, each answered prayer, hospital visit, youth ministry class, outreach event, is an opportunity to thank those that gave and let them know what happened because of their generosity. Do not stop saying thank you.

But do not feel guilty for asking either. Remember, money can either say "worship me" or "give me." When you help people give, you are helping break the bonds of greed and materialism that say "worship me." You set people free to experience the joy of giving. Ask with confidence, knowing how God has used generosity in your own life and with the excited anticipation of how God may use it in the lives of others. "There is no fear in love. But perfect love drives out fear..." (1 John 4:18). Let God's love empower you and drive you as you invite others to join you in the exciting ministry of giving.

Spiritual Fruit Inventory: Giving vs. Worshiping

Love: John 3:16 reminds us, "For God so loved the world that he gave his one and only Son, that whoever believes in him shall not perish but have eternal life." Is your giving reflecting God's love and sharing God's love with others? Who or where is one place you could share God's love through your generosity in the coming month?

Joy: 2 Corinthians 9:7 declares, "Each one must give as he has decided in his heart, not reluctantly or under compulsion, for God loves a cheerful giver." Does giving bring you joy? Are there any areas where you notice a reluctance to give? Spend some time processing those with the Lord. What might need to change?

Peace: Do you feel at peace when you give money away or does it make you anxious? Explore those emotions. If there is a fear of not having enough, talk with God about it and ask for that peace that surpasses all understanding as you align your finances and giving with God's Word.

Patience: Are you patient to see the fruit of your giving? Are you giving with strings attached, or do you surrender each gift, trusting God for the ultimate results once you have followed His leading to give?

Kindness: Where could you share God's kindness through the blessing of generosity, perhaps somewhere it is least expected?

Goodness: Where have you seen God's goodness to provide when you have said yes to the Lord's nudge to give? "Every good and perfect gift is from above, coming down from the Father of the heavenly lights..." (James 1:17 NIV). How can you share God's goodness with others through your generosity, giving God the credit as the source of the gift?

Faithfulness: Where do you need to be faithful to God's prompting to give?

Gentleness: Is your giving characterized by a gentle humility, or do you need the recognition and praise for your gifts?

Self-control: Do you have a system for setting aside money for giving as a first priority? If not, what tool (automatic giving, a separate bank account for giving, donor advised fund, etc.) will you use to make it a first priority?

God, I could never out give You! Thank you for generously supplying all my needs and inviting me into the joy of giving to share what You have provided with others. You do not need my money, but You want my heart, and where my treasure is, there my heart will be also. So, I choose to put You first in my finances, by giving to advance the name of Jesus, not my own name.

Forgive me for the ways I have worshiped money more than I have worshiped You. Forgive me for the ways I have sought credit for my gifts, seeking the approval of others, when You are the source of every good gift. I humbly repent and ask for your help as I seek You first in all areas of my life. I choose to trust You and surrender all I have to You.

POSTLUDE

Blessings

The Lord is moving in miraculous ways, do you see it? God Almighty is blessing you even now, do you notice it? God's favor is upon you, do you walk like it?

Trust and receive all God's plans for you—the Lord's manifold blessings. Listen and be free of the distractions, the trappings of this world. Shift your gaze from material wealth and things to the Provider, the Source of all Life.

Every good gift comes from above. Count off the many things God has given you. List them. Count them one by one. They are more numerous than you can remember. Just marvel in the sheer vastness of God's goodness.

Then, remember how small you are. You are one of billions of people alive right now, not to mention all those who have lived since the creation of the world. In the grand scheme of things, you are insignificant, even if you have an impressive title and accolades. Yet the Creator made you, knows you by name, knows everything you have ever thought or said or done or will do, loves you completely, and has chosen to bless you this much. Receive this blessing from the Lord ...

I desire faithfulness and obedience over sacrifice. Surrender all you have and all you are, and watch what I will do. I will open the floodgates of Heaven and pour out a blessing so vast that none can contain it. Watch what happens as you faithfully follow Me. When you seek Me first, everything else will align. It will not make sense at first, but I desire your whole heart. When you surrender to Me, that is when I can really use you. Watch what happens as you obey My word and listen to My counsel for your wealth. Trust and you will see Me provide when you least expect it and in ways that surprise you. I am not limited by human conditions. I am God. There is none like Me. I have chosen to love you. Receive My love in the many ways I will show you. I love you unconditionally. Receive My love and know that I am the Sovereign Lord. Worship Me and none other.

Other Titles

from Market Square Books

marketsquarebooks.com

Understanding Jesus in the 21st Century

Michael Dent

Being the Church in a Post-Pandemic World

Kay Kotan

Cultural Competency

Partnering with Your Neighbors

Paul Nixon

Church Ecology

Ken Willard & Kelly Brown

Grow Your Church

with these books from Market Square

marketsquarebooks.com

More Titles

from Market Square Books

marketsquarebooks.com

Dream Like Jesus
Bring the Impossible to Life
Rebekah Simon-Peter

Expanding the Expedition
Through Church Partnerships
Christian Coon

The Methodist Story
Volume 2 ▪ 1792-2019
Dr. Donald W. Haynes

Launching Leaders
Leadership Development
Kay Kotan and Phil Schroeder

From Rosario Picardo and Jason Moore